GCSE AQA B: Science in Context
Core Science
The Workbook

This book is for anyone doing **GCSE AQA B Core Science**.

It's full of **tricky questions**... each one designed to make you **sweat** — because that's the only way you'll get any **better**.

There are questions to see **what facts** you know. There are questions to see how well you can **apply those facts**. And there are questions to see what you know about **how science works**.

It's also got some daft bits in to try and make the whole experience at least vaguely entertaining for you.

What CGP is all about

Our sole aim here at CGP is to produce the highest quality books — carefully written, immaculately presented and dangerously close to being funny.

Then we work our socks off to get them out to you — at the cheapest possible prices.

Contents

SECTION 1.1 — MY WIDER WORLD

The Universe 1
The Origin of the Universe 2
The Earth's Structure 3
The Earth's Atmosphere 5
Atoms 7
The Periodic Table 8
Electron Shells 9
Compounds, Mixtures and Formulas 11
Balancing Equations 13
Useful Chemicals From The Ground 14
Getting Metals From Rocks 15
Impacts of Metal Extraction 16
Resources From The Air 17
Economics of Chemical Production 18

SECTION 1.2 — LIFE ON OUR PLANET

Classification 19
Competition and Distribution 20
Adaptations in Animals 21
Adaptations in Plants and Microorganisms 22
Evolution 23
Plant Growth 24
Food Chains and Nutrient Cycling 25
Energy Transfer 27
Pyramids of Biomass and Number 29
The Carbon Cycle 30
Mixed Questions for Sections 1.1 and 1.2 32

SECTION 2.1 — MY FAMILY

The Nervous System 36
Reflexes 37
Hearing 38
Homeostasis 39
Hormones and Blood Sugar 40
Chemicals and Hazards 42
Acids and Alkalis 43
Reactions of Acids 44
Indigestion Tablets and Drug Testing 46
Genes and Chromosomes 48
Variation in Plants and Animals 49
Alleles and Genetic Disorders 51
Treating Genetic Disorders 53

SECTION 2.2 — MY HOME

Limestone 54
Metals 55
Polymers 57
Ceramics 59
Composites 60
Choosing Materials for a Product 61
Fuels from Crude Oil 64
Problems with Fuels from Crude Oil 65
Alternatives to Fossil Fuels 66
Comparing Energy Resources 70
Generating Electricity 71
Supplying Electricity 72

Section 2.3 — My Property

- Calculating Power and Current 73
- Calculating Energy Use and Costs 74
- Efficiency 76
- Energy Labels 77
- Sankey Diagrams 78
- Electromagnetic Waves 79
- The Wave Equation 80
- Uses of Radio Waves and Microwaves 81
- Uses of Infrared, Ultraviolet and Visible Light 82
- Dangers of Electromagnetic Radiation 83
- Mixed Questions for Sections 2.1-2.3 84

Section 3.1 — Improving Health and Wellbeing

- Microorganisms and Disease 88
- The Body's Defence Systems 89
- Vaccination 90
- Use of Drugs to Treat Disease 91
- Antibiotic Resistance and Drug Testing 92
- Recreational Drugs 93
- Medical Uses of Radiation 95
- Radiation Safety Precautions and Ethics 96

Section 3.2 — Developing and Improving Products

- Electroplating 97
- Uses and Risks of Electroplating 98
- New Products 99
- Selective Breeding 101
- Tissue Culture and Cloning 102
- Genetic Engineering 103

Section 3.3 — Environmental Concerns

- Greenhouse Gases 104
- Global Warming and The Kyoto Agreement 105
- Pollution 106
- Pollution and Indicator Species 107
- Waste Disposal and Plastics 108
- Heat Loss in the Home 109
- Reducing Heat Loss in the Home 110
- Pollutants in the Home 111
- Domestic Boilers 112
- Mixed Questions for Sections 3.1-3.3 113

Published by CGP

Editors:
Luke Antieul, Ellen Bowness, Katherine Craig, Emma Elder, Murray Hamilton,
Edmund Robinson, Jane Sawers, Hayley Thompson, Karen Wells.

Contributors:
Mike Dagless, Paddy Gannon, Judith Hayes, Derek Harvey, Frederick Langridge,
Barbara Mascetti, Andy Rankin, Philip Rushworth, Claire Ruthven, Sidney Stringer
Community School, Sophie Watkins.

ISBN: 978 1 84762 601 1

With thanks to Ian Francis, David Hickinson, Jamie Sinclair and Dawn Wright
for the proofreading.
With thanks to Laura Stoney for the copyright research.

Energy Efficiency Label on page 77 © European Union, 1995-2010

Every effort has been made to locate copyright holders and obtain permission to reproduce sources. For those sources where it has been difficult to trace the originator of the work, we would be grateful for information. If any copyright holder would like us to make an amendment to the acknowledgements, please notify us and we will gladly update the book at the next reprint. Thank you.

Groovy website: www.cgpbooks.co.uk

Printed by Elanders Ltd, Newcastle upon Tyne.
Jolly bits of clipart from CorelDRAW®

Based on the classic CGP style created by Richard Parsons.

Psst... photocopying this Workbook isn't allowed, even if you've got a CLA licence. Luckily, it's dead cheap, easy and quick to order more copies from CGP — just call us on 0870 750 1242. Phew!
Text, design, layout and original illustrations © Coordination Group Publications Ltd. (CGP) 2011
All rights reserved.

Section 1.1 — My Wider World

The Universe

Q1 Astronomers study all parts of the Universe.

Circle the correct words in each sentence to describe the different parts of the Universe.

a) The Sun is a **star** / **galaxy**.

b) The Sun and eight planets make up the **Solar System** / **Milky Way**.

c) The Milky Way is a **Solar System** / **galaxy**.

d) The Universe contains **many galaxies** / **one galaxy**.

e) The **Sun** / **Moon** is at the centre of our Solar System.

f) The Earth **is** / **is not** at the centre of the Universe.

Q2 Josie has written a list of facts about **telescopes** to learn, but some of the facts are wrong.

Tick the boxes to show the **two** true statements in Josie's list.

Telescopes are only used to observe the Earth's atmosphere. ☐

X-ray telescopes are based on Earth. ☐

Telescopes are used to observe how the Universe is changing. ☐

Radio telescopes measure visible light. ☐

Telescopes can be used to make observations from space. ☐

Q3 Julie and Adam set up **optical telescopes**. Julie sets up her telescope on top of a **mountain**. Adam sets up his telescope at the bottom of a **valley**.

a) What do optical telescopes detect?
Circle your answer.

radio waves   **visible light**

  X-rays

b) i) Who has chosen the better location for their telescope? Circle your answer.

  Julie   **Adam**

ii) Explain your answer to part **i)**.

....

....

....

The Origin of the Universe

Q1 The **Big Bang** is the most accepted theory for the origin of the Universe.

Complete this passage using the words below.

> expanding   matter   energy   expand   explosion

Many scientists believe that all the .... and .... that created the Universe started in one small space. There was a huge .... and the material started to .... The Universe is still ....

Q2 Brian is an alien. He likes to stand on his planet and watch the spaceships take off.

The diagram on the right shows the sound waves from the spaceship **before it takes off**.

When the spaceship takes off it **moves away** from Brian.
Tick the boxes to show whether these statements are **true** or **false**.

                                                                                                                      True False

a) As the spaceship moves away, the length of the sound waves will seem to change.

b) As the spaceship moves away from Brian, the frequency will seem constant.

Q3 The diagram below shows a light spectrum from a **nearby star**.

A spectrum is the rainbow of light produced when white light passes through a prism.

shorter wavelength light   longer wavelength light (red end)

black lines

a) i) How would you expect the spectrum to be different for a star further away?

....

ii) What is this effect called?

....

b) Circle the correct words in the passage below to explain how this supports the idea that the Universe is expanding.

The further away the galaxy, the **greater / smaller** the change in the spectrum. This tells us that more distant galaxies are moving away from us at a **faster / slower** rate than nearer ones.

Section 1.1 — My Wider World

The Earth's Structure

Q1 **Geologists** study the surface of the Earth.

Complete the passage using some of the words from the box.

| tectonic | currents | slowly | quickly | plates | convection |

The surface of the Earth is made up of ....

These usually move around very .... over time. However, some

changes to the Earth's surface happen very .... The movement is

caused by .... in the mantle.

Q2 The diagram shows the Earth's structure. Label the **crust**, **mantle**, **atmosphere** and **core**.

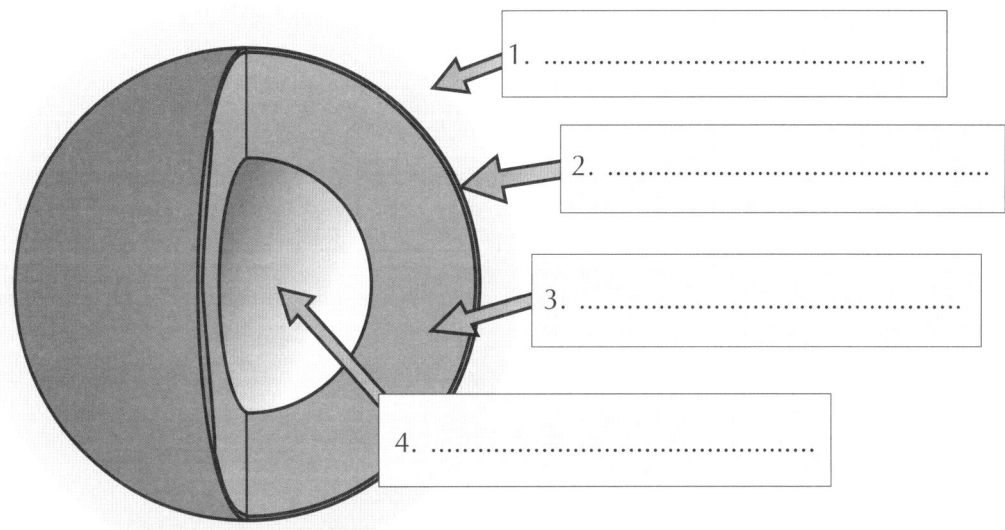

1. ....
2. ....
3. ....
4. ....

Q3 **Match up** the description to the key phrase or word.

Crust — Often form where two tectonic plates meet and molten rock rises up near the surface

Mantle — Caused by sudden movements of plates

Convection current — Caused by radioactive decay in the mantle

Tectonic plates — Thinnest of the Earth's layers

Volcanoes — Slowly flowing layer that plates float on

Earthquakes — Large pieces of crust and upper mantle

Section 1.1 — My Wider World

The Earth's Structure

Q4 The map on the left shows where most of the world's **earthquakes** take place. The map on the right shows the **tectonic plates**.

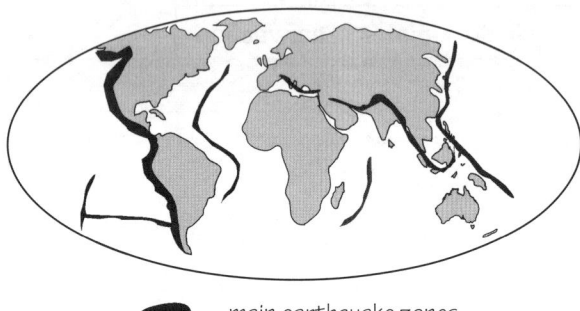
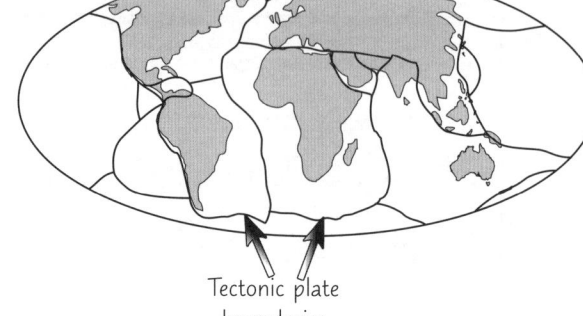

= main earthquake zones

Tectonic plate boundaries

Compare the two maps.
What do you notice about the main earthquake zones?

....

Q5 Fleur studies **earthquakes**. She's looking at the boundary between the African and Arabian plates.

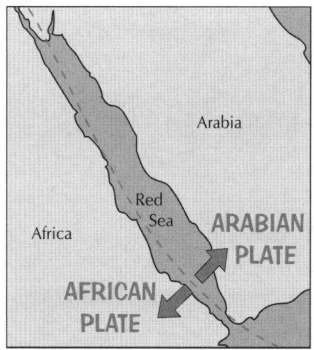

Fleur finds that the Red Sea is getting wider at a speed of **1.6 cm per year**.

a) If the sea level and rate of plate movement stays the same, how much will the Red Sea widen in **10 000** years?

Remember to include a unit in your answer.

....

....

b) The Red Sea is exactly **2000 m** wide at a certain point. If the sea level and rate of plate movement remain the same, how wide will the Red Sea be at this point in **5000** years' time?

....

....

c) The sudden movement of tectonic plates can lead to earthquakes.
Name **one other** event that is caused by tectonic plate movement.

....

Section 1.1 — My Wider World

The Earth's Atmosphere

Q1 Tick the boxes to show whether the following statements about the **first billion years** of the Earth's existence are true or false.

True False

a) Cooling over time has caused the Earth's surface to change.

b) Violent volcanic activity removed carbon dioxide from the atmosphere.

c) Plants and algae produced the first oxygen by photosynthesis.

Q2 The table below shows the gases which make up **volcanic gases**, and the gases which make up the **atmosphere today**. Use the table to answer the questions below.

Gas	% in volcanic gases	% in atmosphere
nitrogen	5	78
oxygen	0	21
carbon dioxide	11	0.04
water vapour	20	0 – 0.07

a) Which gas makes up most of the atmosphere today?

....

b) Which gas present in the atmosphere today could **not** have come from volcanoes?

....

c) Which gas released by volcanoes created the oceans?

....

d) Name **two other** gases which were present in the early atmosphere.

1. .... 2. ....

Q3 The graph shows the percentages of two gases in the **atmosphere** over the last four billion years.

a) What is Gas A? Circle the correct answer.

oxygen   **carbon dioxide**

b) What is Gas B? Circle the correct answer.

oxygen   **carbon dioxide**

c) What **process**, involving plants, has lowered the percentage of Gas B in the atmosphere?

....

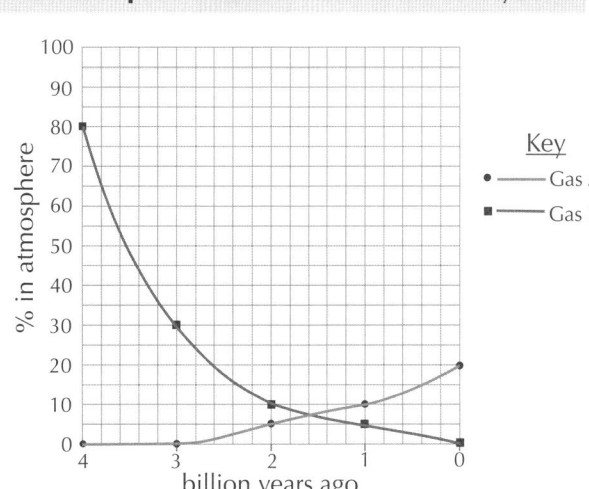

Section 1.1 — My Wider World

The Earth's Atmosphere

Q4 Carbon dioxide and methane in the atmosphere help to keep the Earth warm.

a) What is the name given to gases in the atmosphere which keep the Earth warm?

....

b) Put the following statements in order by numbering them 1 to 4 to show how the gases keep the Earth warm.

This radiation warms the Earth's surface.	☐
Carbon dioxide and methane absorb most of this heat and reflect it back towards Earth.	☐
Radiation from the sun is allowed to pass through the Earth's atmosphere.	☐
The Earth reflects radiation back into space.	☐

c) Why is it important that the Earth is kept warm?

....

Q5 The Earth's temperature is a **balance** between the heat radiation it gets from the **sun** and the heat it **reflects** back into space.

a) Circle the correct words to complete these sentences.

i) Radiation from the sun is **short wave / long wave** radiation.

ii) The Earth reflects heat back into space as **short wave / long wave** radiation.

iii) Greenhouse gases absorb **short wave / long wave** radiation.

b) Complete the diagram by showing the **path of the radiation** from the sun after it enters the atmosphere.

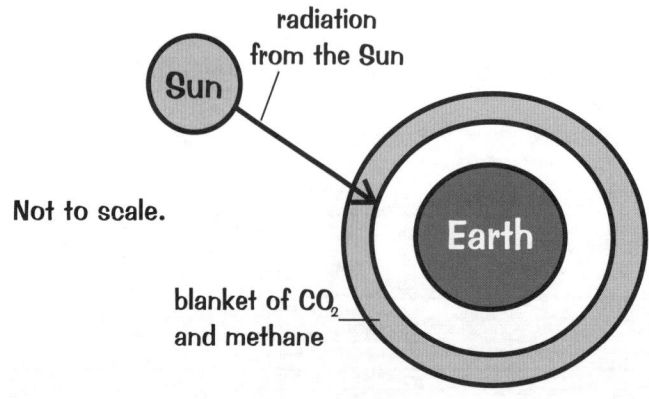

Top Tips: Hopefully you haven't found this page too tricky and are totally happy with how carbon dioxide and methane in the atmosphere keep the Earth warm. Make sure you know how the magic happens — learning the process above will make it all crystal clear.

Section 1.1 — My Wider World

Atoms

Q1 George is a **scuba diving** instructor. When he goes diving he takes a bottle of **oxygen** so that he can breathe underwater.

Label an **electron** and the **nucleus** on this diagram of an oxygen atom.

a) ....

b) ....

Q2 **Draw lines** to match up the statements below to the parts of an atom that they describe.

These have no charge.	Electrons
These are positively charged particles.	Protons
These move around the nucleus in shells.	Neutrons

Q3 Katya tests **fizzy mineral water** to make sure there are no harmful chemicals in it.

Draw lines to show whether the substances Katya has found are **atoms**, **molecules** or **ions**.

H—O—H Mg^{2+}
Zn   Atoms   O—C—O
         Molecules Ca^{2+}
H^+ Ions

Q4 Alice is learning about the different **elements**.

a) What is an element?

....

....

b) Elements can be represented by **names** or by one or two letter **symbols**. Circle all of the **elements** below.

CH_4 K   Gold   Lead   Water   Boron
CO_2 O_2 Sodium chloride

Section 1.1 — My Wider World

The Periodic Table

Q1 Look at the table below and then answer the questions.

Element	Atomic number	Mass number
Sodium	11	23
Magnesium	12	24
Aluminium	13	27

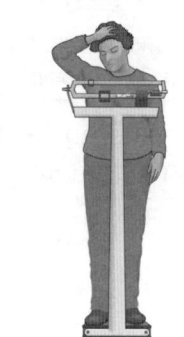

Julie didn't like the look of her mass number.

a) i) What does an element's atomic number show?

....

ii) What does an element's mass number show?

....

b) Circle the correct answer to complete the sentences below.

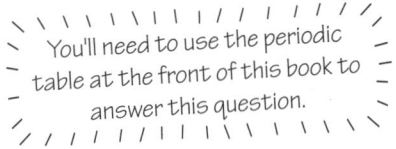

Use the atomic and mass numbers for the elements in the table above to work these out.

i) Sodium has **10 / 11 / 12 / 23** protons.

ii) Magnesium has **10 / 11 / 12 / 24** neutrons and **10 / 11 / 12 / 24** electrons.

iii) Aluminium has **13 / 14 / 27 / 28** neutrons.

iv) An atom of sodium has **more / less** protons than an atom of aluminium.

Q2 Laurence has a part-time job helping Professor Bumble in his laboratory. The professor gives Laurence a list of **elements** to brush up on.

a) Fill in the table with the missing **elements** and **chemical symbols** from Professor Bumble's list.

b) Fill in the table box to show the element **atomic numbers** and **mass numbers** of the elements.

You'll need to use the periodic table at the front of this book to answer this question.

Element	Chemical symbol	Atomic number	Mass number
Oxygen			
Hydrogen			
Chlorine			
Lead			
Silver			
	Au		
	B		
	Fe		
	N		
	Si		

Section 1.1 — My Wider World

Electron Shells

Q1 a) Tick the boxes to show whether each statement is **true** or **false**.

    True False

  i) Electrons always occupy shells in atoms. ☐ ☐

  ii) The shells nearest the nucleus are always filled first. ☐ ☐

  iii) Atoms are most stable when they have partially filled shells. ☐ ☐

  iv) Atoms are more likely to react when they have full outer shells. ☐ ☐

b) How many electrons are allowed in:

  i) The first shell?

  ....

  ii) The second shell?

  ....

  iii) The third shell?

  ....

Q2 Andrew was asked to draw the electron arrangement of **neon**. Describe **two** things that are wrong with his diagram.

1. ....

....

2. ....

....

Q3 Fill in the table with the **electron arrangement** for the following elements. The first one has been done for you.

Element	Electron arrangement
Beryllium	2, 2
Oxygen	
Silicon	
Magnesium	
Aluminium	
Argon	

You'll need to use the periodic table (see inside front cover) to work out how many electrons each element has.

Section 1.1 — My Wider World

Electron Shells

Q4 **Chlorine** is used in swimming pools to clean the water. It has an **atomic number** of 17.

a) What is its electron arrangement? ....

b) Draw the electrons on the shells in the diagram.

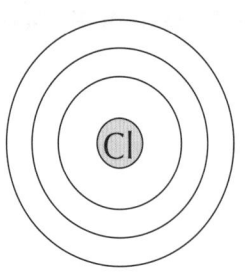

Q5 Draw the **full electron arrangement** for these elements. (The first three have been done for you.)

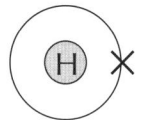   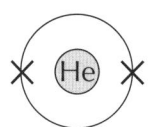   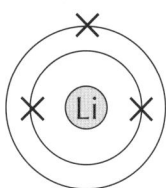

Hydrogen   Helium   Lithium

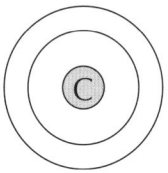   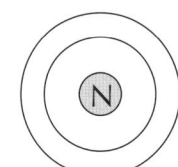   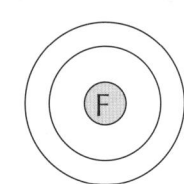

a) Carbon   b) Nitrogen   c) Fluorine

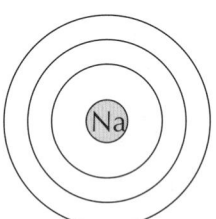   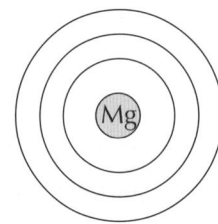   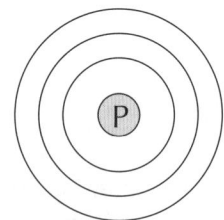

d) Sodium   e) Magnesium   f) Phosphorus

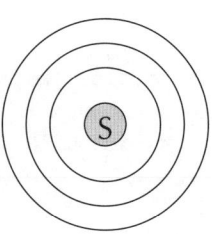   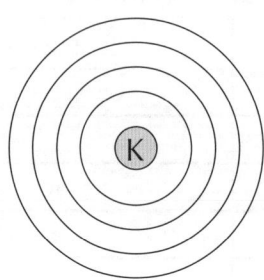   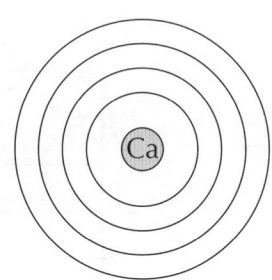

g) Sulfur   h) Potassium   i) Calcium

Section 1.1 — My Wider World

Compounds, Mixtures and Formulas

Q1 Tick the boxes to show whether the statements are **true** or **false**.

    True False

a) Mixtures contain different types of atoms bonded together chemically. ☐ ☐

b) A compound has to be made up of just one type of atom. ☐ ☐

c) The atoms in a compound are bonded together chemically. ☐ ☐

d) Mixtures are easier to separate than compounds. ☐ ☐

Q2 Farouk has drawn diagrams to represent **compounds** and **mixtures**. Complete the sentences below with the letter of the correct diagram.

a) Mixture ....

b) Compound .... and ....

Q3 Crude oil contains lots of **different substances** which aren't bonded together. Most of them contain carbon joined to hydrogen — for example pentane (C_5H_{12}) and octane (C_8H_{18}). Crude oil also contains some sulfur.

a) Tick the boxes to show whether the substances are compounds, mixtures or neither.

	Compound	Mixture	Neither
Crude oil	☐	☐	☐
Octane	☐	☐	☐
Pentane	☐	☐	☐
Sulfur	☐	☐	☐

b) Is it **easier** to separate pentane or crude oil? Explain your answer.

....

....

Section 1.1 — My Wider World

Compounds, Mixtures and Formulas

Q4 Simon is a **weatherman**. Every day he produces a report on the **air quality** at the weather station where he works.

Write the names of the following compounds that Simon finds in an air sample.

a) CO_2 ....

b) H_2O ....

c) CH_4 ....

d) NH_3 ....

Q5 A word equation shows the substances taking part in a reaction. For example, the equation below shows how calcium and oxygen react to form calcium oxide:

$$\text{calcium} + \text{oxygen} \rightarrow \text{calcium oxide}$$

Complete the following sentences by circling the correct word in each pair.

a) In a chemical equation, everything on the left-hand side of the arrow is a **product / reactant**, and everything on the right-hand side is a **product / reactant**.

b) The properties of the products are **similar to / different from** the properties of the reactants.

Q6 Draw lines to match up the **compounds** below to their **formulas**.

hydrogen chloride	Al(OH)$_3$
magnesium hydroxide	NaHCO$_3$
sodium bicarbonate	HCl
aluminium hydroxide	CaCO$_3$
calcium hydroxide	Ca(OH)$_2$
calcium carbonate	Mg(OH)$_2$

Top Tips: If you're still struggling to get your head around chemical formulas then try and break them down a bit. For example, anything that's a hydroxide will always have 'OH' in its formula and a carbonate will have 'CO$_3$'. Then you just need to spot the symbol of the element it's bonded to.

Section 1.1 — My Wider World

Balancing Equations

Q1 Fill in the blanks using some of the words below to complete the passage.

mass	arranged	balanced	number

In chemical reactions, atoms are not lost or gained — they're just .... differently. Chemical equations have to be .... so that the .... of each type of atom is the same on both sides. As the number of atoms is the same on both sides of the equation, the .... of the reactants and the products is always the same.

Q2 Katy is a chemist. She needs to make **aluminium sulfide**.
The equation for making aluminium sulfide is:

$$\text{aluminium} + \text{sulfur} \rightarrow \text{aluminium sulfide}$$

a) Aluminium sulfide has the formula Al_2S_3. Write a balanced symbol equation for the reaction.

....

b) Katy needs to make **3 kg** of aluminium sulfide. She has **1080 g** of aluminium. How much **sulfur** will she use?

....

....

Q3 Only one of the equations below is **balanced correctly**. Circle the one correctly balanced equation.

$Na + O_2 \rightarrow Na_2O$

$Na + O_2 \rightarrow Na_2O_2$

$2Na + O_2 \rightarrow Na_2O$

$4Na + O_2 \rightarrow 2Na_2O$

Q4 **Balance** the following equations by putting numbers in front of the chemicals where necessary.

a) $Zn + HCl \rightarrow ZnCl_2 + H_2$

b) $Fe + Cl_2 \rightarrow FeCl_3$

c) $K + H_2O \rightarrow KOH + H_2$

d) $Al + O_2 \rightarrow Al_2O_3$

Section 1.1 — My Wider World

Useful Chemicals From The Ground

Q1 Lots of useful materials we use come from the **ground**.

a) Circle the four materials below that can be used straight from the ground.

marble   gold   steel   glass
petrol   cement   limestone   sulfur   iron ore

b) Name two methods we can use to take these materials from the ground.

1. ....   2. ....

Q2 Mr Nelson is a science teacher. He is teaching his pupils about **rock salt**.

a) What are the two materials that make up rock salt?

....

b) How is rock salt separated to produce refined salt?

....

....

....

Q3 Gillian works for an **oil company**. She has been asked to give a presentation to school children to explain **how** and **why** we use the fractions in **crude oil**.

a) What is the name of the **process** that separates the fractions in crude oil?

....

b) The notes Gillian prepared for her presentation have been dropped and jumbled up. Write the numbers 1-4 in the boxes to show the correct order of the sentences.

   A   The different fractions in the crude oil condense at different temperatures.

   B   Crude oil is formed from the buried remains of animals and plants. It is extracted from the ground by drilling.

   C   The different chemicals are collected from different parts of the column — the bottom of the column is the hottest, and the top of the column is coolest.

   D   The crude oil is heated until it evaporates, and the gases rise up the column.

c) The different fractions in crude oil are all made up of different sized **hydrocarbons**. Complete the following sentences by circling the correct word in each pair.

   i) The shorter the hydrocarbon molecules, the **lower / higher** the boiling point of the fraction.

   ii) The longer the hydrocarbon molecules, the **less / more** viscous the fraction is.

Section 1.1 — My Wider World

Getting Metals From Rocks

Q1 Joseph carries out an experiment in his science class to see which metals can be **extracted** from their ores using **carbon**.

a) Circle the correct answer to complete the following sentences.

   i) Metal ores are often an oxide of the metal — the metal is bonded to **oxygen / carbon dioxide**.

   ii) Some metals can be extracted from their ores by heating with a **purifying / reducing** agent.

   iii) Only metals which are **less / more** reactive than carbon can be extracted by heating with carbon.

b) Joseph extracts lead from lead oxide by heating lead oxide with carbon.

   i) Write a word equation for this reaction.

   ....

   ii) What is the **reducing agent** used in part **i)**?

   ....

c) Joseph writes a report about the extraction of iron from iron oxide using carbon monoxide. Write the numbers 1-3 in the boxes to put the following word equations for the reaction in order.

   Order

   iron oxide + carbon monoxide → iron + carbon dioxide   ☐

   carbon + oxygen → carbon dioxide   ☐

   carbon dioxide + carbon → carbon monoxide   ☐

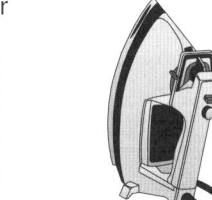

d) Balance the symbol equations for the extraction of lead and iron from their ores.

$$.... PbO + C \rightarrow .... Pb + CO_2$$

$$Fe_2O_3 + ... CO \rightarrow .... Fe + ... CO_2$$

(Higher only)

Q2 **Electrolysis** is used to separate aluminium from its ore.

a) Why can aluminium **not** be extracted from its ore by heating it with carbon?

....

b) What state must the ore be in before electrolysis can be carried out?

....

c) Why is electrolysis an **expensive** process?

....

Section 1.1 — My Wider World

Impacts of Metal Extraction

Q1 Fill in the blanks using the words below to complete the passage about **phytomining**.

| harsh | roots | phytomining | burnt | ash | recovered | soil |

When coal and metal mines are no longer used, bits of metal may be left in the .... These metals are .... from the affected areas by .... Plants are grown and take up the metals from the soil using their .... These plants are then harvested and ...., and the metal is removed from the .... Only plants which are able to survive the .... conditions can be used.

Q2 Melanie works for a metal producer at a **copper mine** in Africa. Copper ore is removed from the mine, and **copper** is extracted from its ore.

a) At the moment, the mine sends the copper ore to the UK for the copper to be extracted. Suggest one reason why transporting large amounts of copper ore like this is bad for:

   i) the **company**.

   ....

   ....

   ii) the **environment**.

   ....

   ....

b) Melanie is writing a report about the possibility of expanding the mine so more copper ore can be mined locally.

   i) Suggest how this could benefit the **local people**.

   ....

   ....

   ii) Suggest why this might be bad for the **environment**.

   ....

   ....

Section 1.1 — My Wider World

Resources From The Air

Q1 John has to make a presentation to his class about air.
He remembers that air is a **mixture** of gases, but can't remember which ones.

a) What are the three main gases in air?

1. ....

2. ....

3. ....

b) i) What method can be used to separate the gases in air?

....

ii) What **property** of the different gases in the air means they can be separated in this way?

....

Q2 Complete the passage below by choosing the correct words from each pair.

> The gases in air can be separated by cooling air until it **liquefies / solidifies**, at -200 °C. During this cooling, water vapour **condenses / evaporates** and is removed. Carbon dioxide freezes and is removed. The remaining air is then gradually warmed. Nitrogen has a lower boiling point than oxygen so this boils off **first / last** while the oxygen remains **liquid / a gas**. Once nitrogen and oxygen have been separated, another fractionating column is used to separate the remaining gases.

Q3 **Argon**, **helium** and **nitrogen** are all used in **industry**.

Draw lines to match the gases to their uses.

balloons   argon   fertiliser

to make ammonia   helium   electrical discharge tubes

nitrogen   light bulbs

Section 1.1 — My Wider World

Economics of Chemical Production

Q1 Mike is the manager of a **chemical company** that produces **cleaning products**.

a) Why is it important that Mike makes sure that the company makes as much **product** as possible from the raw materials they use?

....

....

b) Hydrogen peroxide can be explosive. **40 kg** of hydrogen peroxide is needed to make a batch of **bleach**. Suggest **two reasons** why Mike wouldn't buy a lot more hydrogen peroxide than needed.

1. ....

2. ....

Q2 Brian is responsible for choosing the **manufacturing process** for a new floor polish — 'In the Buff'.

The table below outlines four different processes (A, B, C and D) that could be used to make 'In the Buff'.

Process	Raw materials cost (£m)	Running costs (£m)	Waste produced (tonnes)	Product (tonnes)
A	10	11	8	550
B	5	11	6	600
C	21	7	3	480
D	13	9	7	520

a) Which process has the highest **costs**?

....

b) Why may the company want to **avoid** a process which produces lots of waste?

....

c) Brian chooses process B. Explain why he has made a good choice.

....

....

Section 1.1 — My Wider World

Section 1.2 — Life On Our Planet

Classification

Q1 Dr. Dare is recording the differences between plants and animals. Put crosses in the correct columns to say which characteristics refer to which **group of organisms**.

	Plant	Animal
Travels to new places		
Makes its own food		
Is fixed to the ground		

Q2 Use the words below to **fill in** the **gaps** and complete the passage about classification.

Each word can only be used once.

similar	name	identify	kingdoms	groups	physical

Classification is about putting organisms that are .... into .... Living things are divided into .... based on their .... characteristics. All scientists use the same classification system because it makes it easier to .... and .... organisms.

Q3 In the 1700s Linnaeus developed a **classification model** based on what organisms looked like. Since then, there have been other models of classification. The models have been **updated** several times.

Tick **two** boxes below which give correct reasons why the models have been updated.

Scientists have found a system which can classify every organism without any doubt. ☐

Scientific developments mean we know more about how organisms are related. ☐

Scientists found that not every organism fitted neatly into the groups proposed by old models. ☐

The study of the behaviour of organisms has shown that no organisms are related. ☐

Andy always updates his model...

Competition and Distribution

Q1 Plants and animals live in forests. To survive they need certain resources.

a) **Draw lines** to connect the boxes to show which resources are essential for plants, essential for animals and essential for both.

Light

Nutrients from the soil

Space

Plants

Animals

Water

Shelter

Food

Mates

b) Tick the box next to the statement that **best describes** competition.

☐ Organisms compete for resources when there are not enough to go around.

☐ Organisms compete for resources when there are more resources than they need.

☐ Organisms only compete for resources with members of their own species.

Q2 Larry is puzzled about why his favourite type of bird is only found in some parts of the UK. Suggest how the following factors could affect the **distribution** of the birds.

a) Resources ....

....

b) Competition ....

....

c) Environmental conditions ....

....

d) Predators ....

....

Top Tips: Competition for resources is serious stuff. Grey and red squirrels need the same resources to survive. When the greys were introduced to the UK they were so much better at getting the stuff they needed that lots of the reds died. Now red squirrels are really rare.

Section 1.2 — Life On Our Planet

Adaptations in Animals

Q1 Tina is learning about adaptations in animals at school.

a) Describe what **adaptations** are.

....

b) Complete the passage using the words given.

heat	strong	sweat	water	small	body fat

Mammals living in deserts need to make sure they lose as little ....
as possible. They make .... amounts of very .... urine.
They also produce very little .... They keep cool in other ways,
e.g. their thin layer of .... helps them to lose .... easily.

Q2 Ashley is researching how **camels** are adapted to live in deserts.

a) Describe the **harsh conditions** in the deserts where camels live.

....

b) Explain how a camel's **hump** is a special adaptation for desert life.

....

....

....

Q3 Pictures of a **polar bear** and a small rodent called a **kangaroo rat** are shown below. Complete the sentences below by circling the correct words.

Diagrams are not to scale.

a) The **polar bear** / **kangaroo rat** has the biggest surface area.

b) The **polar bear** / **kangaroo rat** has the biggest surface area compared to volume.

c) Having a smaller surface area compared to volume means that **more** / **less** heat is lost from an animal's body.

Section 1.2 — Life On Our Planet

Adaptations in Plants and Microorganisms

Q1 Scott works at a research station in the Arctic. He was surprised to learn that there were **microorganisms** living in such an **extreme environment**.

a) Circle the correct word below to show the name given to microorganisms that can live in extreme environments.

Extremophobes   **Extremophiles**   **Decomposers**   **Chemophiles**

b) Microorganisms can live in the following extreme environments. Suggest what conditions make these places extreme.

　i) Arctic regions

　..

　ii) Volcanic vents

　..

　iii) Desert regions

　..

c) Suggest one other example of extreme conditions that microorganisms can survive in.

....

Q2 The picture shows a **cactus** plant. It is **adapted** to living in desert conditions.

Explain how each of the following features of the cactus help it to survive in its normal habitat.

a) Surface area

....
....

b) Stem

....
....

c) Roots

....
....

Section 1.2 — Life On Our Planet

Evolution

Q1 The theory of evolution by **natural selection** was developed by Charles Darwin. Tick the sentences below that describe aspects of natural selection correctly.

- [ ] There are differences within species that are caused by differences in their genes.
- [ ] Genes aren't different enough within species to make members of the same species look different.
- [ ] The best adapted animals and plants are most likely to survive.
- [ ] Some characteristics are passed on through breeding from parent to offspring.
- [ ] Animals that have successfully adapted do not need to produce offspring.

Q2 Emily has drawn a diagram to show the **evolutionary relationships** of four different species.

Dolphins   Mice   Rays   Sharks

Evolutionary relationships show how living things are related. Ecological relationships show how living things interact.

a) Tick the box next to the pair of species below that has the most recent common ancestor.

- [ ] Mice and Rays.
- [ ] Rays and Sharks.
- [ ] Mice and Sharks.

b) Sharks and dolphins share similar characteristics even though they are not closely related. Suggest **one** thing this could tell us about their ecological relationship.

....

Q3 The buff tip moth looks like a **broken stick**. This makes it hard to see when it's on a plant. The statements below describe how this feature might have evolved. Write numbers in the boxes to show the order the statements should be in.

- [ ] Ancestors to the buff tip moth showed variation in their appearance. Some had genes that made them look a bit like a stick.
- [ ] So the stick-like moths were more likely to survive and reproduce.
- [ ] Genes that made the moths look like sticks were more likely to be passed on to the next generation.
- [ ] Some birds couldn't see the stick-like moths.

Section 1.2 — Life On Our Planet

Plant Growth

Q1 Some **plants** were grown in a lab to study the effect of **light** on their growth. The diagram shows the shape of each shoot before the experiment and after the experiment had ended.

a) Circle the correct name given to the response of plants to light.

    auxins   phototropism   photosynthesis   gravitropism

b) Which **part** of the plant shoot is most sensitive to light?

....

c) Which plant hormone controls the growth of the tip?

....

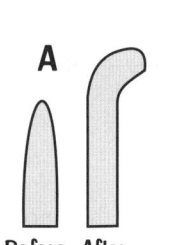
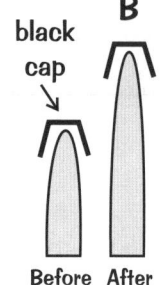
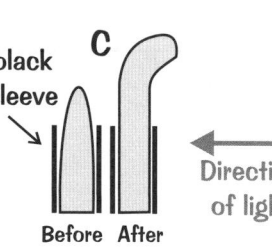

d) On each picture, shade in the region that contains the most of this hormone.

e) Give three other factors that can affect the growth of plants.

1. ....

2. ....

3. ....

Q2 Ivy did an experiment to study how **growth hormones** change the **direction** that **shoots** and **roots** grow in. The two diagrams show the shoot and root.

a) Complete the diagrams below to show which way the root or shoot **will grow**. Then, select the **correct word** from each pair to explain your answers.

i)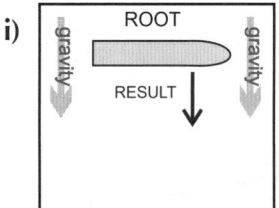

Explanation: A root growing sideways will have more auxin on its

upper / lower side, causing the upper / lower side to grow more

slowly / quickly. This means the root bends upwards / downwards.

ii)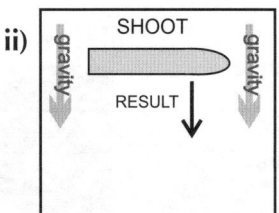

Explanation: A shoot growing sideways will have more auxin on its

upper / lower side, causing the upper / lower side to grow more

slowly / quickly. This means the shoot bends upwards / downwards.

b) What is the name given to the response of plants to gravity?

....

Section 1.2 — Life On Our Planet

Food Chains and Nutrient Cycling

Q1 The **food chain** below is part of a countryside **ecosystem**.

wheat → cockroaches → frogs → foxes

a) Draw lines to match three of the organisms in this food chain to their role in the food chain.

frogs   producer
wheat   secondary consumer
cockroaches   primary consumer

b) Describe what a food chain shows.

....

....

c) Describe what is meant by the following terms.

i) Ecosystem ....

....

ii) Biosphere ....

....

Q2 Robin is training to be a forest ranger. He's studying the **flow** of **energy** through **food chains**.

a) Circle the correct word to show the source of energy in food chains.

humans   microorganisms   the sun

b) Circle the correct word to show what energy is stored as once it has entered the food chain.

a pyramid   biomass   faeces

c) Describe how energy passes through each stage of the food chain.

....

....

Section 1.2 — Life On Our Planet

Food Chains and Nutrient Cycling

Q3 Indicate whether these statements are **true** or **false**.

                                                                                                                             True False

a) Sunlight is important for all food chains.

b) Each stage in a food chain is called a consumer.

c) Materials are not lost from food chains — they are recycled.

d) In food chains, producers eat consumers.

e) Energy only is passed between the steps of food chains.

Q4 Clarice **recycles** the waste from her kitchen. The waste is broken down by microorganisms.

a) State the name given to microorganisms that break down the waste material.

    ....

b) Name three conditions needed for the microorganisms to work best.

    1. ....

    2. ....

    3. ....

Q5 The sentences below describe how **elements** are **recycled** in a food chain. Sort them into the correct order by numbering them 1 to 5. The first one has been done for you.

a) ☐ The elements they contain are released.

     [1] Plants take up minerals from the soil.

     ☐ Nutrients in plants are passed to animals through feeding.

     ☐ Waste and dead tissues are decayed by microorganisms.

     ☐ They turn these minerals into plant material.

b) Circle the correct words to complete the following sentences.

    i) Nutrients can be recycled **five** / **many** times.

    ii) Recycled materials are returned to the soil by **decay** / **digestion**.

Top Tips: It's a bit of a shocker but recycling isn't a new fad — the world around us has been doing it since the year dot. Basically, just make sure you know your stuff on food chains, where energy comes from and the conditions microorganisms need for decomposition and you'll be fine. Groovy.

Section 1.2 — Life On Our Planet

Energy Transfer

Q1 Complete the sentences below by circling the correct words.

a) Material and energy are **lost / gained** at each stage of the food chain.

b) Animals and plants release energy through the process of **photosynthesis / respiration**.

c) Material and energy is lost in the food chain through **faeces / eating**.

d) Some of the energy is **gained / lost** through **growth / heat**.

e) Faeces contain material that can't be **digested / decomposed**.

Q2 The diagram shows a farm **food chain**.

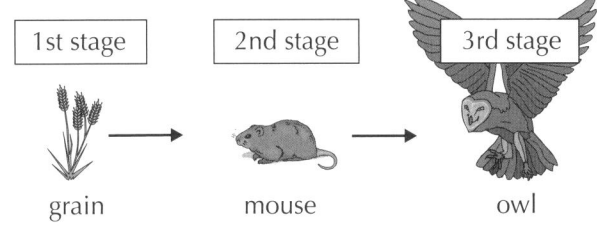

a) Put the following amounts of energy stored under the correct organisms.

500 kJ, 50 000 kJ, 8000 kJ

b) Calculate the amount of energy lost between the:

i) 1st and 2nd stages. ....

ii) 2nd and 3rd stage. ....

c) Explain what happens to the energy in an owl that dies.

....

Q3 The diagram shows the **energy transfer** in a dairy farm food web.

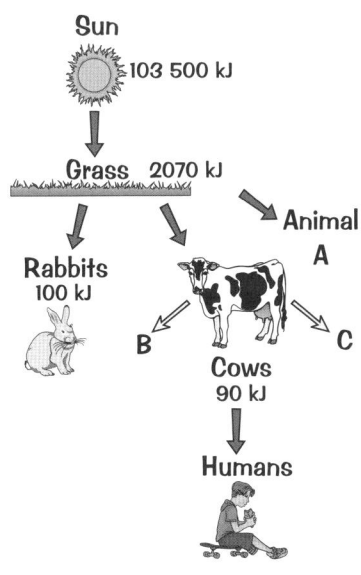

a) Using the figures shown on the diagram, work out the percentage of the Sun's energy that is available in the grass.

....

b) The efficiency of energy transfer from the grass to the next stage is 10%. Work out how much energy is available in animal A.

....

....

c) **B** and **C** are processes that represent energy loss. Suggest what these processes might be.

....

d) Explain why food chains rarely have more than five stages.

....

....

Section 1.2 — Life On Our Planet

Energy Transfer

Q4 The table shows a **food chain** in a garden.

	lettuce	Caterpillar	small bird	large bird
1	10 kJ	100 kJ	5000 kJ	30 000 kJ
2	30 000 kJ	30 000 kJ	30 000 kJ	30 000 kJ
3	30 000 kJ	5000 kJ	100 kJ	10 kJ

leaf it out

a) Which row, 1, 2 or 3, shows the amount of energy available at each trophic level? ....

b) Circle the answer below that shows how much energy is available to the caterpillar in the food that it eats.

5000 kJ   25 000 kJ   30 000 kJ

c) Circle the answer below that shows how much energy is lost from the caterpillar to the small bird.

100 kJ   4900 kJ   5000 kJ

Q5 A **food chain** is shown below.

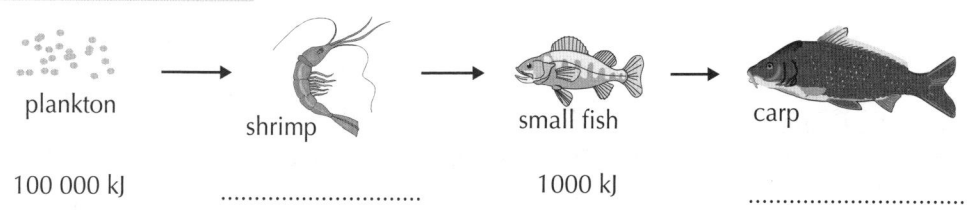

plankton → shrimp → small fish → carp

100 000 kJ   ....   1000 kJ   ....

a) 90 000 kJ is lost between the 1st trophic level (plankton) and the 2nd trophic level (shrimp).

i) On the diagram, write the amount of energy available in the shrimp for the small fish.

ii) Calculate the **efficiency** of energy transfer from the 1st to the 2nd trophic level.

....

b) The energy transfer from the small fish to the carp is **5%** efficient.

i) On the diagram, write the amount of **energy** available in the **carp**.

ii) How much energy is **lost** from the food chain at this stage?

Don't forget to take a calculator into the exam.

....

Top Tips: It's all too easy to get muddled over units when you're talking about energy transfer. Remember that kJ stands for kilojoules (1000 joules) and that efficiencies are usually given as percentages — don't go saying the efficiency of the energy transfer from the worms to the birds is 15 J.

Section 1.2 — Life On Our Planet

Pyramids of Biomass and Number

Q1 The **pyramid of biomass** below describes a seashore food chain.

a) Which organism is the producer?

....

b) Which organism is the primary consumer?

....

c) Which stage has the greatest biomass?

....

crab
winkle
algae

Q2 A single **robin** has a mass of 15 g and eats caterpillars. Each robin eats 25 **caterpillars** that each have a mass of 2 g. The caterpillars feed on 10 **stinging nettles** that together have a mass of 500 g. Study the pyramid diagrams shown then answer the questions that follow.

A **B** **C** **D**

a) Describe what each stage of a pyramid of biomass represents.

....

b) Which is most likely to represent a pyramid of **biomass** for these organisms?   ....

c) Explain how you decided on your answer to part **a)** above.

....

Q3 **20 ladybirds** eat **100 insects** which feed on an **oak tree**.

a) **Sketch** a pyramid of **number** for the food chain in the box.

b) Explain the unusual shape of this pyramid.

....

....

Top Tips:
If you're asked to draw a pyramid of biomass in the exam, check if you need to draw it to scale. Don't lose marks because you haven't read the question properly. Remember — pyramids of biomass almost always end up pyramid-shaped with producers having the most biomass.

Section 1.2 — Life On Our Planet

The Carbon Cycle

Q1 Carbon is cycled between the atmosphere, animals and plants all the time. Complete the diagram below as instructed to show a **part** of the **carbon cycle**.

CO$_2$ in the air

plant   animal

a) Add an arrow or arrows labelled **P** to represent **photosynthesis**.

b) Add an arrow or arrows labelled **R** to represent **respiration**.

c) Add an arrow or arrows labelled **F** to represent **feeding**.

Q2 Answer the following questions to show how the **stages** in the **carbon cycle** are ordered.

a) Number the sentences below to show how carbon moves between the air and living things.

.... Animals eat the carbon compounds in plants and algae.

...1......... Carbon dioxide in the air.

.... Plants, algae and animals die.

.... Plants and algae take in carbon dioxide for photosynthesis and make carbon compounds.

b) Add a point 5 to complete the cycle and show how carbon in dead organisms is returned to the air.

Point 5: ....

....

Q3 Plants are an important part of the **carbon cycle**.

a) Give the name of the process in plants that removes carbon dioxide from the atmosphere.

....

b) What products do plants convert this carbon dioxide into?

....

c) How is the carbon in plants passed on through the food chain?

....

Section 1.2 — Life On Our Planet

The Carbon Cycle

Q4 Indicate whether these statements are **true** or **false**.

a) The carbon in sea water comes from dissolved carbon dioxide.

b) Marine animals and plankton take carbon from the sea water and use it to make shells and bones.

c) Over really long periods of time, the bones and shells of dead organisms form calcium carbonate.

d) Carbon is stored as limestone for very short periods of time.

e) Limestone is formed from organisms including coral.

f) Limestone is formed from organisms that are found in cold, deep oceans.

Q5 The diagram below shows one version of the **carbon cycle**.

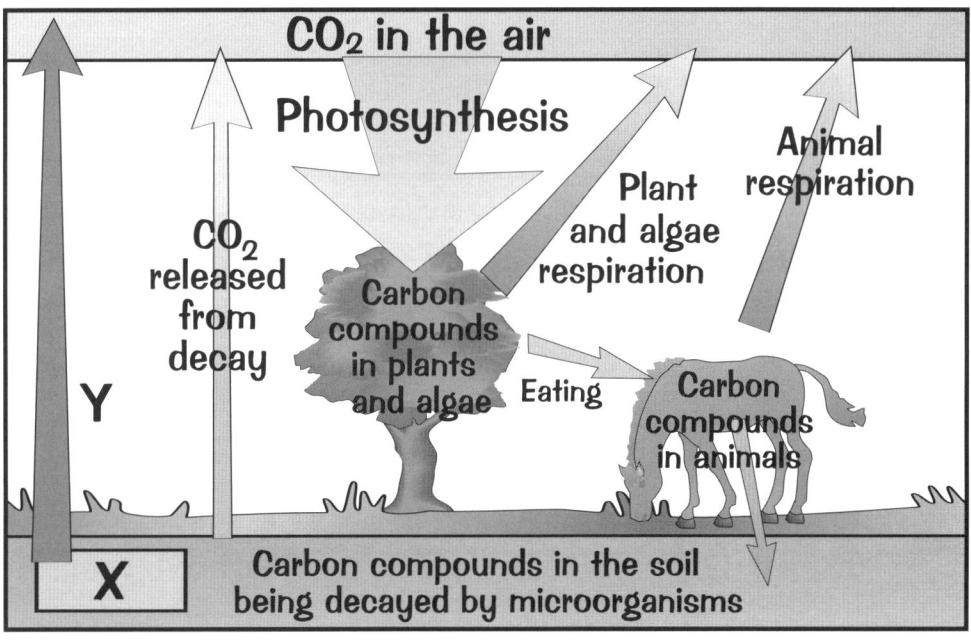

a) Name substance **X** shown on the diagram above. ....

b) Explain why substance **X** contains carbon.

....

....

c) Name the process labelled **Y** on the diagram above. ....

Section 1.2 — Life On Our Planet

Mixed Questions for Sections 1.1 and 1.2

Q1 Metals make up about **80%** of all the elements in the periodic table.

a) Shade the area where **metals** are found on this periodic table:

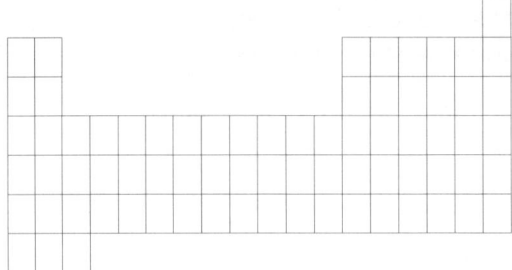

b) Below are three elements from the periodic table. Fill in the boxes with their electron arrangements.

Q2 The graphs below give information about the Earth's atmosphere millions of years ago and today.

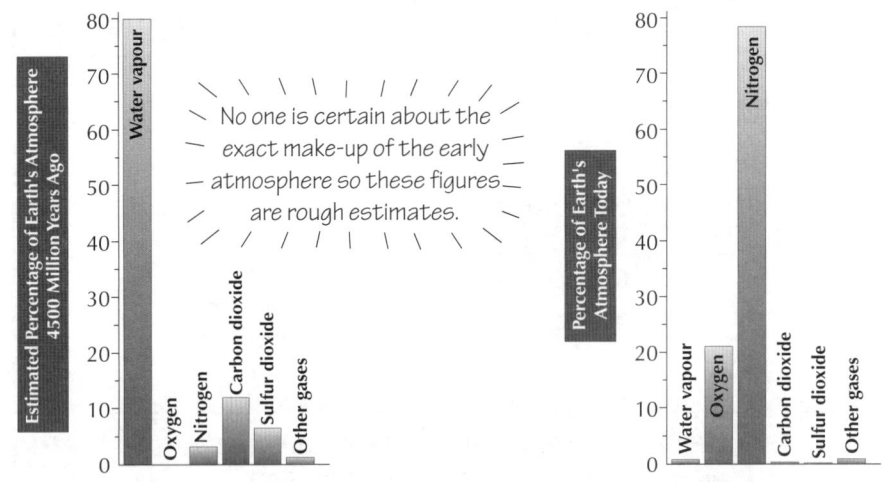

a) What released the gases that formed the early atmosphere?

....

b) What percentage of the Earth's atmosphere today is oxygen? ....

c) Name two types of **organisms** that caused an increase in oxygen and a decrease in carbon dioxide.

1. .... 2. ....

d) Fill in the gaps to describe each of the following substances as an **element**, **compound** or **mixture**.

i) Air .... iii) Oxygen ....

ii) Methane .... iv) Carbon dioxide ....

Section 1.2 — Life On Our Planet

Mixed Questions for Sections 1.1 and 1.2

Q3 Danielle works for a company who process copper ore to make **pure copper**. She uses the process of **electrolysis** to make the pure copper.

a) Name the **method** used to remove copper ore from the ground.

....

b) Give two reasons why removal of copper from the ground may be bad for the environment.

1. ....

2. ....

c) Tick the boxes to indicate if the following statements are true or false: **True   False**

   i) Electrolysis is used to extract metals less reactive than carbon.   ☐ ☐

   ii) Electrolysis only works if the ore is molten (liquid).   ☐ ☐

   iii) Electrolysis can also be used to extract the different gases in air.   ☐ ☐

d) Danielle finds a way to produce more copper by electrolysis using the same amount of copper ore. Explain why this is good for the company.

....

....

Q4 Ben has bought himself a new **optical telescope**.

a) Ben uses the telescope to look at a galaxy. Tick **one** of the boxes below next to the correct explanation for why the image he sees is not very clear.

☐ The Earth's atmosphere blocks some of the light coming from objects in space.

☐ Optical telescopes can only be used in space.

b) Ben has been told that when stars **move away** from the Earth, the **wavelength** and **frequency** of the light they give out seems to change. What is the name given to this effect?

....

c) Ben says "red-shift evidence supports the **Big Bang** theory". Is he right? Explain your answer.

....

....

....

Section 1.2 — Life On Our Planet

Mixed Questions for Sections 1.1 and 1.2

Q5 A new type of **desert organism** has been discovered by Professor Smith.

a) Professor Smith thinks the organism belongs to the **animal kingdom**.
Give two characteristics shared by members of the animal kingdom.

1. ....

2. ....

b) Explain why it is important to have an international system for classification of organisms.

....

....

c) Suggest how the following characteristics help the animal to survive in desert conditions.

i) Very thin layer of body fat.

....

ii) Doesn't sweat very much.

....

Q6 *Awesomus plantus* is a **desert plant**. Most **fossilised** examples of *Awesomus plantus* have **shallow roots**. **Today** most plants have **deep roots** which make them better able to get water.

a) Use the theory of **natural selection** to explain this change.

....

....

....

....

b) A gardener who lives in Wales decides to grow *Awesomus plantus* in two different conditions.

i) Tick the set of conditions you would expect the plants to grow the most in.

☐ 1. In a greenhouse where the heating and lights are always kept on.

☐ 2. Outside in his garden.

ii) Explain your answer.

....

....

Mixed Questions for Sections 1.1 and 1.2

Q7 The diagram below shows a **food chain** observed on the savannahs of Tanzania. It also shows the amount of **energy** available in each trophic level.

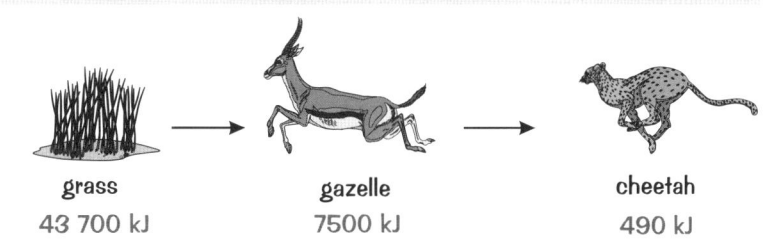

grass — 43 700 kJ → gazelle — 7500 kJ → cheetah — 490 kJ

a) i) How much energy is lost from the 1st trophic level (grass) to the next (gazelle)?

....

ii) Calculate the efficiency of this energy transfer.

....

b) Suggest two ways in which energy might be lost by the gazelle.

1. ....

2. ....

c) **Carbon** also moves through the food chain. It is continuously being **recycled** from one form to another as the diagram below shows.

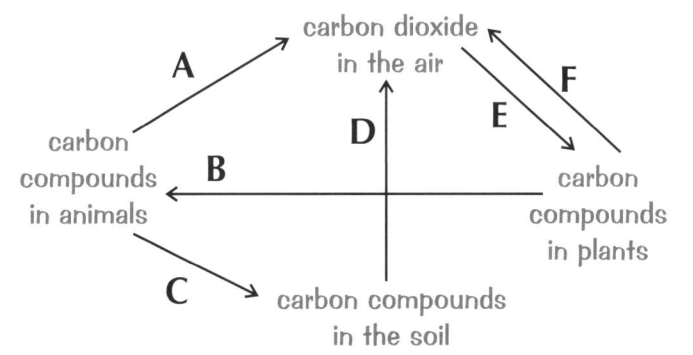

Diagram labels: carbon compounds in animals, carbon dioxide in the air, carbon compounds in plants, carbon compounds in the soil. Arrows labelled A, B, C, D, E, F.

Box: respiration, feeding, photosynthesis, respiration by decomposers, decomposition, respiration

Use the words in the box to name the processes labelled **A**, **B**, **C**, **D**, **E** and **F** in the diagram.

A .... B ....

C .... D ....

E .... F ....

d) Cheetahs don't always eat all of the meat on a gazelle. What is not eaten begins to **decompose**. Give **three** conditions that are needed for decomposition.

1. ....

2. ....

3. ....

Section 1.2 — Life On Our Planet

The Nervous System

Q1 **Sense organs** contain **receptors**. In each sentence below, underline the sense organ involved and write down the type of receptor it contains.

a) Tariq puts a piece of lemon on his tongue.

....

b) Liz covers her nose as she smells something nasty.

....

c) Lindsey hides her eyes during a scary film.

....

d) Xabi's ears were filled with the sound of the crowd cheering.

....

e) Name two other types of sense receptor.

1. ....   2. ....

Q2 John has suffered **damage** to his **spinal cord**. His doctor says it has been completely severed. The diagram shows the position of the damage.

a) The **spinal cord** is part of the nervous system. What is the function of the nervous system?

....

b) Complete the passage about the nervous system by circling the correct word from each pair.

> When John touches a sharp object, a **stimulus / response** is detected
>
> by **effectors / receptors** in his skin. These send **information / chemicals**
>
> along **sensory / motor** neurones to his brain. His brain processes
>
> the information and sends it along **sensory / motor** neurones to muscles
>
> in the arm. These muscles can then bring about an appropriate response.

c) Suggest **how** the injury to John's spinal cord will affect his movements.

....

Reflexes

Q1 Ian steps on a pin and has a **reflex reaction**. Circle the correct answer to complete each of the following sentences about reflex reactions.

a) Reflexes happen more **quickly** / **slowly** than responses you have to think about.

b) The **sense receptors** / **nervous system** can coordinate a reflex response.

c) The main purpose of a reflex is to **protect** / **display** the body.

d) Reflexes happen **with** / **without** you thinking about them.

e) A **reflex arc** / **CNS** is the pathway information takes to get from a receptor to an effector.

Q2 Name three types of **neurone** involved in a reflex action.

1. ....

2. ....

3. ....

Q3 Jenny walks from a **dark** room out into bright **sunlight**. Look carefully at the diagrams below.

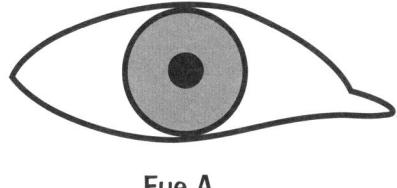

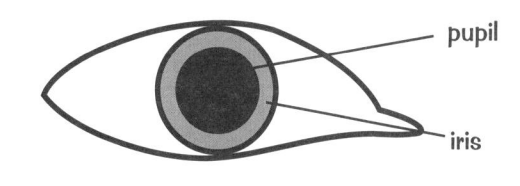

Eye A   Eye B (pupil, iris labelled)

a) When light receptors in the eye detect an increase in the amount of light, the pupil becomes smaller. This is a **reflex response**.

   i) Describe the difference you can see in the appearance of the two eyes.

   ....

   ii) Which diagram do you think shows Jenny's eye in bright sunlight? Explain your answer.

   ....
   ....

b) Suggest why it is an advantage to have a reflex response controlling the action of the eye.

   ....
   ....
   ....

Section 2.1 — My Family

Hearing

Q1 Sound waves are caused by **vibrating** objects.

a) Put the following sentences in the correct order to describe how the sound of a drumbeat is made and reaches our ears.

    A   The vibration of the drum sets the air molecules next to it vibrating too.

    B   We hear the sound when the vibrations reach our ears.

    C   When someone beats a drum, the skin on top of the drum vibrates.

    D   The vibrations in the air travel outwards as a wave.

Correct order: .... , ... , ... , ...

b) Circle the correct word to show what type of waves sound waves are.

    longitudinal waves   transverse waves   inverse waves

Q2 The table below shows the frequency of some sounds recorded by Nadine.

a) Complete the table by circling 'yes' or 'no' to show if the sound can be **heard** by humans.

Sound	Frequency (Hertz)	Can it be heard?
Bat sonar	25 000-80 000	i) yes / no
Flying hummingbird	90	ii) yes / no
Low elephant call	15	iii) yes / no
Piano — middle C	262	iv) yes / no
Heartbeat	1-2	v) yes / no
Dog whistle	22 000	vi) yes / no
Violin — top note	3136	vii) yes / no

b) Nadine goes nightclubbing a lot. She takes an ear test and finds that she's lost some of her hearing. Suggest how her hearing could have been damaged.

....

....

Top Tips: Lots of things around us are so noisy that if we listened to them for long enough they'd damage our ears — for example, pneumatic drills and jet engines. But even your MP3 player can damage your hearing if you have the volume turned up too high — so be careful with that dial.

Section 2.1 — My Family

Homeostasis

Q1 Define **homeostasis**.

....

Q2 Yolanda and Subarna are on holiday in **Spain**, where the daytime **temperature** can get very **high**.

a) Yolanda and Subarna notice that they are sweating more than usual. They are told that the blood vessels supplying their skin capillaries dilate in the heat.

Tick the boxes to show whether these statements are **true** or **false**.   True   False

i) When water in sweat evaporates, it carries heat away with it. ☐ ☐

ii) More heat is lost to the surroundings when the blood vessels supplying the skin capillaries are smaller in diameter. ☐ ☐

iii) Sweating causes your body to retain heat. ☐ ☐

b) Which part of the body identifies an increase in the temperature of the blood?

....

Q3 A rescue team discovered an injured climber on a mountain ledge. The rescue team were concerned that the mountaineer had a very **low body temperature**.

a) When you are cold, your blood vessels change in order to help maintain body temperature. Circle the correct words in the passage below to describe how.

> When you are too cold, blood vessels close to the skin's surface **dilate** / **constrict**. This means that **more** / **less** blood gets to the surface of the skin. This stops the blood from **losing heat to** / **gaining heat from** the surroundings.

b) The climber's internal body temperature is returned to normal by **negative feedback**. Describe how negative feedback works.

....

....

....

....

Section 2.1 — My Family

Hormones and Blood Sugar

Q1 Jack has a condition caused by having too much growth hormone. His doctor is explaining how **hormones function**. Complete the passage below using the following words.

glands	target	blood	chemicals

Hormones are .... that are produced in ....

They are released directly into the .... They travel all

over the body but only affect .... organs.

Q2 Ruby and Paul both have diabetes, so they need to **monitor** and **control** their glucose levels carefully.

a) Give one symptom of diabetes.

....

b) Diabetes is caused when the body can't make a particular hormone, or respond to that hormone. What is the name of that hormone?

....

c) Describe how Type 1 and Type 2 diabetics **control** their blood sugar levels.

Type 1 ....

Type 2 ....

d) More and more people are getting Type 2 diabetes.
Suggest an implication of this for the NHS (National Health Service).

....

Q3 *(Higher only)* Danny runs a three mile race. At the end of the race the level of **glucose** in his **blood** is **low**.

a) **Circle** the correct words in the following paragraph to explain what happens.

> The **pancreas / liver** detects glucose loss in blood. The pancreas **releases / detects** a hormone. The liver converts stored **soluble / insoluble** glycogen to **glucose / insulin**. Glucose is added to the **blood / pancreas**.

b) What is the name of the hormone that is released when blood sugar is low?

....

Section 2.1 — My Family

Hormones and Blood Sugar

Q4 A research scientist is investigating the effect of diet on blood glucose levels. The graph below shows the levels of **glucose** in the blood for two different people after they had both eaten exactly the same type of meal.

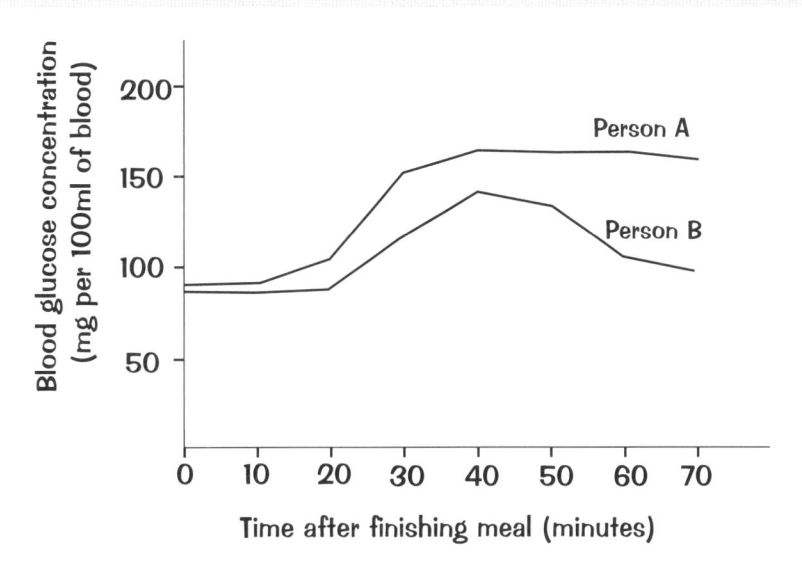

a) Insulin controls the levels of glucose in the blood. What in the body is insulin produced?

....

b) When did the blood sugar level of person B start to decrease?

....

c) Number the stages (1 - 4) to show one way in which blood sugar levels decrease.

☐ The pancreas releases insulin.

☐ A rise in glucose level detected by pancreas.

☐ Glucose is stored as glycogen.

☐ Insulin causes the liver to take up glucose from blood.

d) Why was it important to ensure that both people in this experiment ate the same meal before measurements of blood sugar were taken?

....

....

Top Tips: Although diabetes is a serious disease, many diabetics are able to control their blood sugar levels. They're able to carry on with normal lives and do most of the things they want. Sir Steve Redgrave even won a gold medal at the Olympics after he had been diagnosed with diabetes.

Section 2.1 — My Family

Chemicals and Hazards

Q1 **Hazardous chemicals** can be labelled to warn people that they are **dangerous**.

a) Draw lines to join up the symbols below with the hazards that they represent.

i) [corrosive symbol]

corrosive

ii) [flame symbol]

radioactive

iii) [radioactive symbol]

highly flammable

You need to know what these symbols mean in the lab and in your exam.

b) The hazard symbols below might be used to label acids. Write down the hazards that they represent.

i) ....   ii) ....

Q2 Draw **hazard symbols** in the boxes below for the following hazards.

a) Oxidising

b) Harmful

Q3 Wearing safety goggles, gloves and a lab coat reduces the risks when working with chemicals. Suggest **two other ways** that you could reduce the risks.

1. ....

2. ....

Top Tips: It's important to remember that these hazard symbols aren't only useful for your exam — they might just save your skin (literally) in the lab or even around your home. That cupboard under the sink in your kitchen is probably packed with more danger than a javelin catching contest...

Section 2.1 — My Family

Acids and Alkalis

Q1 Mick has spilt some **battery acid** on the floor. He decides to see what happens if he pours (alkaline) **oven cleaner** onto the acid.

a) Complete the equation below for the reaction between an acid and an alkali.

acid + alkali → .... + ...

b) Write a symbol equation, including state symbols, to show the reaction in part a) in terms of hydrogen ions and hydroxide ions.

....

c) Circle the correct term for this kind of reaction.

decomposition　　　　oxidation　　　　neutralisation

d) Which of the following ions:

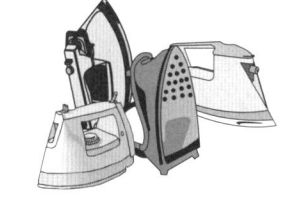

| OH^- | H^- | OH^+ | H^+ |

i) is a positively charged hydrogen ion?　　　.............................

ii) is present in an acidic solution?　　　.............................

iii) is present in an alkaline solution?　　　.............................

iv) would be present in a solution with a pH of 10?　　　.............................

Q2 Ants' stings hurt because of the **formic acid** they release. The pH measurements of some household substances are given in the table.

SUBSTANCE	pH
lemon juice	4
baking soda	9
caustic soda	14
soap powder	11

a) State the pH of a neutral substance. ....

b) i) Give the substance in the table that is most acidic. ....

ii) Give the substance in the table that is most alkaline. ....

c) Suggest a substance from the table that could be used to relieve the discomfort of an ant sting. Explain your answer.

....

....

....

Section 2.1 — My Family

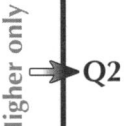

Reactions of Acids

Q1 Metal oxides and hydroxides are neutralised in reactions with acids.

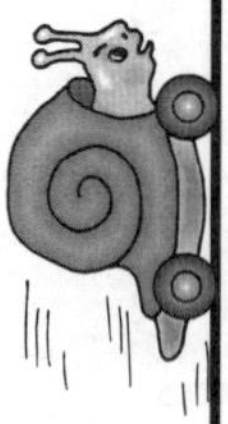

a) Complete the word equation for a reaction between a metal oxide and an acid:

metal oxide + acid → .... + ...

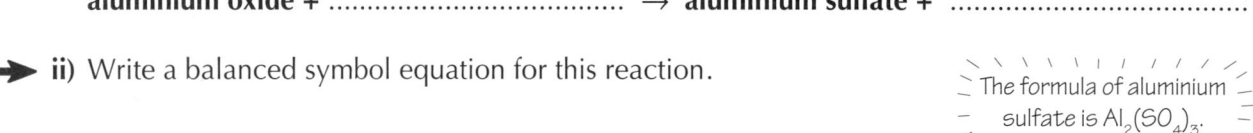

b) Complete the word equation for a reaction between a metal hydroxide and an acid:

metal hydroxide + acid → .... + ...

c) i) Complete the word equation for the reaction between aluminium oxide and sulfuric acid:

aluminium oxide + ... → aluminium sulfate + ...

ii) Write a balanced symbol equation for this reaction.

The formula of aluminium sulfate is $Al_2(SO_4)_3$.

....

d) Zinc oxide also reacts with sulfuric acid. Give the word equation for this reaction.

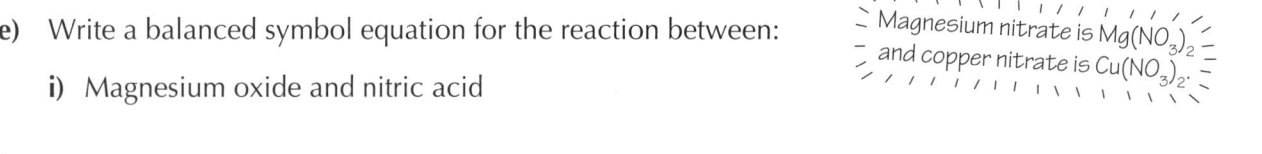

....

e) Write a balanced symbol equation for the reaction between:

Magnesium nitrate is $Mg(NO_3)_2$ and copper nitrate is $Cu(NO_3)_2$.

i) Magnesium oxide and nitric acid

....

ii) Copper oxide and nitric acid

....

Q2 Ronald is writing up some experiments that he did in class. Unfortunately he didn't have time to balance the equations in class.

a) Write out the **balanced** versions of these equations, showing metal hydroxides reacting with acids.

i) $Ca(OH)_2 + HCl \rightarrow CaCl_2 + H_2O$ ....

ii) $KOH + H_2SO_4 \rightarrow K_2SO_4 + H_2O$ ....

b) Hydrobromic acid reacts with magnesium hydroxide as shown in the equation below to form a bromide salt and water.

$$Mg(OH)_2 + 2HBr \rightarrow MgBr_2 + 2H_2O$$

i) Name the salt formed in this reaction. ....

ii) Write a balanced equation for the reaction between aluminium oxide and hydrobromic acid. (The formula of aluminium bromide is $AlBr_3$.)

....

Section 2.1 — My Family

Reactions of Acids

Q3 Jane's chemistry teacher wrote some word equations for **acids** reacting with **metal oxides** and **metal hydroxides** on the white board. The school cleaner accidentally rubbed some of the words off the board. Fill in the missing words to complete the word equations.

a) hydrochloric acid + lead oxide → .... chloride + water

b) nitric acid + potassium hydroxide → potassium .... + water

c) sulfuric acid + copper oxide → copper sulfate + ...

d) hydrochloric acid + ... oxide → nickel .... + ...

e) .... acid + zinc oxide → .... nitrate + ...

f) sulfuric acid + ... hydroxide → sodium .... + ...

Q4 Archie is reacting **acids** with **metal carbonates** in neutralisation reactions.

a) Complete the following word equations.

  i) hydrochloric acid + ... carbonate → copper .... + water + ...

  ii) .... acid + magnesium .... → .... nitrate + ... + carbon dioxide

  iii) sulfuric acid + lithium carbonate → .... + ... + ...

b) Complete and balance the following symbol equations.

  i) .... HCl + CaCO$_3$ → CaCl$_2$ + ... + CO$_2$

  ii) H$_2$SO$_4$ + Na$_2$CO$_3$ → Na$_2$SO$_4$ + ... + ...

  iii) .... HNO$_3$ + ... → Ca(NO$_3$)$_2$ + H$_2$O + CO$_2$

  iv) .... + Na$_2$CO$_3$ → .... NaCl + ... + ...

Top Tips: Don't forget — you only need to be able to balance these equations if you're taking the higher paper. These sorts of questions are easier than they seem at first — you just need to know the patterns that the reactions follow, so stick at it and you'll be an acid boffin (just like me) in no time.

Section 2.1 — My Family

Indigestion Tablets and Drug Testing

Q1 Heartburn is caused by too much **hydrochloric acid** in your stomach.

a) Explain why **acidic** conditions are necessary in the stomach.

....

b) Explain why compounds like calcium carbonate and magnesium hydroxide are used in **antacids**.

....

c) Write a **word equation** showing how calcium carbonate neutralises hydrochloric acid.

....

Q2 Joey wanted to test whether some antacid tablets really do **neutralise acid**.

He dissolved a tablet in some **hydrochloric acid** and tested the **pH** of the solution. Further tests were carried out after dissolving a second, third and fourth tablet. His results are shown in the table below.

Number of Tablets	pH
0	1
1	2
2	3
3	7
4	9

a) Plot a graph of the results.

b) Describe how the pH changes when antacid tablets are added to the acid.

....

c) How many tablets were needed to neutralise the acid?

....

Q3 Ushma is an **animal technician** who works for a pharmaceutical company. She is involved in **testing new medicines** that are being developed by the company.

a) Why is it necessary for drugs to be tested before they can be sold and used by the public?

....

b) Number the following in the correct order to show the usual development and testing process for new drugs.

☐ Live animals   ☐ Human volunteers   ☐ Human tissue

Section 2.1 — My Family

Indigestion Tablets and Drug Testing

Q4   Read the extract below and answer the following questions.

> Animal rights campaigners gathered in Corel Square today to demonstrate against the opening of Froggarts' new animal testing laboratory. This lab carries out the final tests of new drugs on animals to make sure they're safe before they're given to humans.
>
> I interviewed several of the animal rights campaigners, who made their feelings about the company very clear, saying, "Animals are so different from humans that testing on them is pointless", "Why should animals suffer for our benefit?" and "Animal testing shouldn't be used because it hasn't always successfully shown harmful side effects of some drugs".
>
> The head of scientific research at Froggarts pointed out that, "We share over 90% of our DNA with other primates and many other animals have very similar organs to our own, making them good models of the human body". However, he admitted that, "an extremely small number of side effects that humans experience cannot be detected in other organisms, but animal testing is still the safest way to make sure a drug isn't harmful to humans".
>
> In 2005, 395 000 animals were used for safety experiments in the UK. Of these animals, 73% were used for testing the safety of drugs.

a)   How many animals were used for safety experiments in 2005?

    ....

b)   Give two reasons why the animal rights campaigners object to testing new medicines on live animals.

    ....

    ....

c)   Explain why the head of scientific research at Froggart's still thinks that animals are good models to show how a new drug may work in humans.

    ....

    ....

Section 2.1 — My Family

Genes and Chromosomes

Q1 Geneticists study the **genes** and **chromosomes** inside cells.

a) Arrange the following in order of size, giving the smallest first and the largest last:

    gene   cell   chromosome   nucleus

....

b) Tick the boxes to show whether these statements are **true** or **false**.

	True	False
i) Short sections of chromosomes are called genetics.	☐	☐
ii) Each cell contains many genes.	☐	☐
iii) Chromosomes consist of genetic material.	☐	☐
iv) Simple animal cells do not have a nucleus.	☐	☐
v) Genes are found in the cytoplasm.	☐	☐

c) What do genes control?

....

Q2 A geneticist can check an embryo's cells to make sure the chromosomes are normal. The **diagram** below shows an embryo **cell**.

a) Name the parts of the cell labelled A, B and C on the diagram.

A ....
B ....
C ....

b) Which part of the cell, **A**, **B**, or **C**, contains the chromosomes?

....

Top Tips: Make sure that you properly understand this stuff because it's really important in the rest of the section. Unless it's in your genes that you're a genius, then you'd better get learning.

Section 2.1 — My Family

Variation in Plants and Animals

Q1 Mr Brown has **red hair** and Mrs Brown has **black hair**. They have four children.

a) Use the words below to fill in the blanks in the passage to explain why each child will have different characteristics.

genes	mixture	genetic
Some differences in the characteristics of the Brown's children are due to .... causes. The children will have got some of their .... from their mother and some from their father. This .... of different genes from their parents causes the children to look different.

b) Tick the boxes to show whether the following statements about Mr and Mrs Brown's children are **true** or **false**.

    True   False

i) The children will share some characteristics with Mr and Mrs Brown.   ☐ ☐

ii) The children will look like Mr and Mrs Brown because they have exactly the same genes.   ☐ ☐

iii) The combination of genes from two parents causes genetic variation.   ☐ ☐

Q2 Sam, Bob and Alfie are brothers. Alfie is 8 years old. Sam and Bob are both 5 years old and are **identical twins**. Identical twins have identical genes.

a) i) Sam **weighs more** than Bob. Is this difference due to their genes or their environment?

....

ii) Give a reason for your answer.

....

....

Here, these jeans might help your big nose...

b) Suggest **two** of Alfie's characteristics that are likely to be determined by a combination of his genes and his environment.

1. ....

2. ....

c) Circle the **correct word** from each pair to explain why the brothers share certain characteristics.

Alfie / Bob and Sam will share some genes because they

have **the same / different** parents. However, they will share

more / fewer genes than Sam and **Alfie / Bob** do, so there

will be **greater / less** genetic variation between them.

Section 2.1 — My Family

Variation in Plants and Animals

Q3 Al and Mo are brother and sister. The diagram below shows some of their **characteristics**.

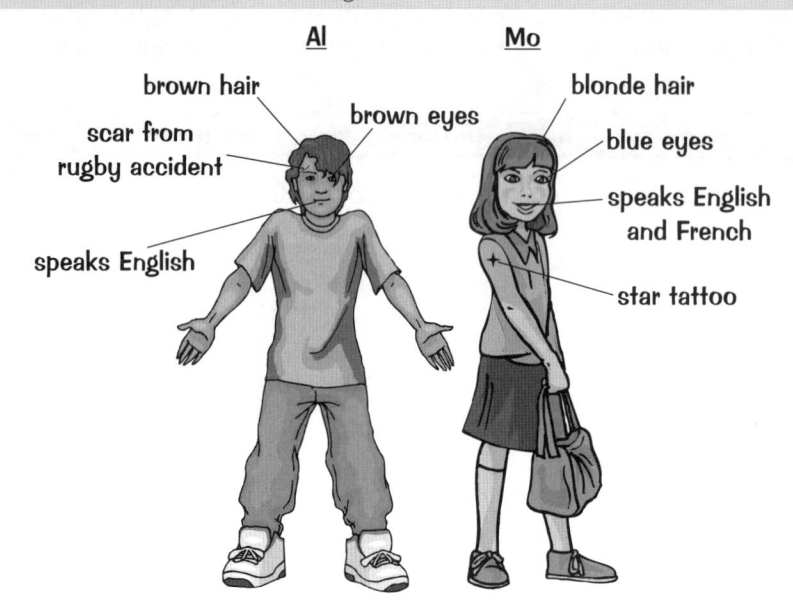

Al — brown hair, brown eyes, scar from rugby accident, speaks English

Mo — blonde hair, blue eyes, speaks English and French, star tattoo

Draw lines to connect the boxes to show which of Al and Mo's characteristics are **genetically** determined and which are **environmentally** determined.

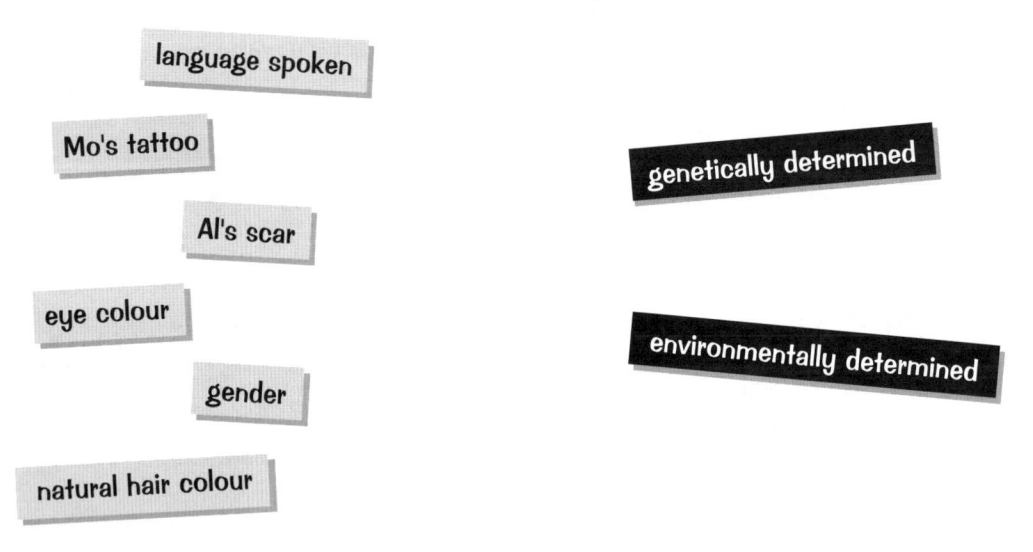

- language spoken
- Mo's tattoo
- Al's scar
- eye colour
- gender
- natural hair colour

genetically determined

environmentally determined

Q4 Susan is growing spider plants and they all look a bit different. Underline the correct word to show whether these **differences** are caused by **genes**, the **environment**, or **both**.

a) Leaf colour. genes / environment / both

b) Presence or absence of spines. genes / environment / both

c) Height. genes / environment / both

d) Caterpillar bite marks. genes / environment / both

Section 2.1 — My Family

Alleles and Genetic Disorders

Q1 Sally is a **geneticist**. She studies people's **genes** to help her understand the way certain characteristics are **inherited** from one generation to the next.

Tick the boxes to show whether the following statements are **true** or **false**.

		True	False
a)	Someone with one recessive allele will not display the characteristic of that allele.	☐	☐
b)	Alleles are different forms of the same gene.	☐	☐
c)	Sickle-cell anaemia, polydactyly and haemophilia are all genetically inherited disorders.	☐	☐
d)	A child of two parents who each have a recessive allele will definitely show the recessive characteristic.	☐	☐

These were once your great-great-great grandfather's.

Q2 David and Helen have three children called Pete, Ruth and Jenny. Pete was born with **cystic fibrosis** but is the only sufferer in his family.

a) **F** is the normal allele and **f** is the **recessive**, faulty allele that causes cystic fibrosis. What combination of alleles does Pete have?

....

b) i) What combination of alleles must David and Helen have? Circle the correct answer.

   FF and Ff   **Ff and Ff**   **FF and FF**   **ff and ff**   **ff and Ff**

ii) Give a reason for your answer.

....

....

c) Jenny grew up to marry Michael. Michael has no history of cystic fibrosis in his family. Tick the answer that correctly describes the chance of them having a child with cystic fibrosis.

Hint: Jenny doesn't have cystic fibrosis, but her brother does.

☐ Impossible — neither Jenny nor Michael is a sufferer.

☐ Possible — they could both have the allele that causes cystic fibrosis.

☐ Possible — Jenny must have the allele that causes cystic fibrosis, so it doesn't matter what alleles Michael has.

Top Tips: Questions on alleles always look more fiddly than they really are. The trick to them is knowing which combination causes the dominant characteristic to show up (two dominant alleles **or** one dominant and one recessive allele) and which combination causes the recessive characteristic to show up (two recessive alleles). If you can remember that they'll be dead easy.

Section 2.1 — My Family

Alleles and Genetic Disorders

Q3 Jimmy is doing a project at school studying fruit flies. The flies usually have **red** eyes but a small number have white eyes. Having **white** eyes is a **recessive** characteristic.

a) Complete the following sentences with either '**red eyes**' or '**white eyes**'.

   i) **R** is the allele for ....

   ii) **r** is the allele for ....

   iii) Fruit flies with alleles **RR** or **Rr** will have ....

   iv) Fruit flies with the alleles **rr** will have ....

b) Two fruit flies have the alleles **rr** and **Rr**. They fall in love and get it on.

   i) Complete this Punnett square to show the possible offspring. One's been done for you.

	parent's alleles	
	R	r
r	Rr	
r		

   (left label: parent's alleles)

   ii) What is the probability that the fruit flies' offspring will have **white eyes**?

   ....

   iii) The fruit flies have 16 offspring. How many of the offspring are **likely** to have **red eyes**?

   ....

Q4 Ben is breeding hamsters. He has some normal and boring ones and some crazy ones. The **allele** that causes craziness is **recessive** (b) and the allele that causes normality is **dominant** (B).

a) Ben wants more normal and boring hamsters so he breeds two together. Complete the Punnett square to show the genetic cross.

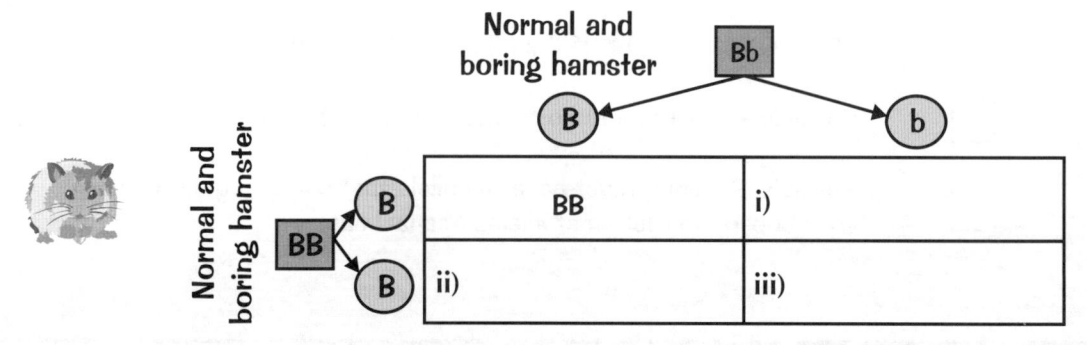

   Normal and boring hamster: Bb → B, b
   Normal and boring hamster: BB → B, B

	B	b
B	BB	i)
B	ii)	iii)

b) Ben ends up with six baby hamsters. How many of them would you expect to be crazy?

....

Section 2.1 — My Family

Treating Genetic Disorders

Q1 A scientist is doing research into two **gene therapy** techniques used to treat cystic fibrosis.

a) Describe what gene therapy is.

....

....

....

b) The scientist treats 100 people with cystic fibrosis using Technique 1 and another 100 with Technique 2. He looks at their side effects and symptoms over 6 months. His results are shown in the table.

Technique	% suffering side effects	% symptom free for 2 months	% symptom free for 6 months	cost (to the hospital) per patient
1	65	76	61	2500
2	32	56	42	1600

i) How many people were symptom-free after six months following Technique 1?

....

ii) Which technique produced the longest lasting results?

....

iii) Why might people decide against this technique even though it produced the longest lasting results in this study?

....

iv) Which technique might a hospital prefer to provide to its patients? Explain your answer.

....

....

c) The scientist has been asked to genetically screen a foetus to see if the unborn baby will have cystic fibrosis. Suggest what issues might be raised by the genetic screening of a foetus.

....

....

....

Top Tips: Don't panic if you're faced with an exam question about some treatment that you've never even heard of before. Just keep cool — you won't be expected to know the details. As long as you can read data from graphs and tables, you'll be absolutely fine.

Section 2.1 — My Family

Section 2.2 — My Home

Limestone

Q1 Mike is a builder. He's been asked to rebuild part of Lancaster Cathedral. To match the rest of the building, Mike decides to use limestone.

a) i) Give the **chemical formula** of limestone.

   ....

   ii) State how limestone is obtained from the ground.

   ....

b) i) Give the **chemical formula** of quicklime.

   ....

   ii) Give the **word equation** of the reaction for the formation of quicklime.

   ....

c) Mike needs to make some **slaked lime** for plastering the walls. Describe how he would make slaked lime from quicklime.

   ....

d) Many of the building materials Mike needs are made using limestone. Circle **three** materials from the ones shown below that are made using limestone.

   glass   paint   bricks   cement   granite   wood   concrete

Q2 Use the words below to fill the gaps in the passage.

| sand | sodium carbonate | mortar | concrete | limestone |

Heating powdered .... with clay in a kiln makes cement. When cement is mixed with water, gravel and sand it makes .... , which is a very common building material. Or, cement can be mixed with sand and water to make .... , which is used to stick bricks together. Heating limestone with .... and .... makes glass.

Metals

Q1 Tick the boxes to show whether these statements are **true** or **false**.

		True	False
a)	Metals are hard and strong.	☐	☐
b)	All metals are poor conductors of heat.	☐	☐
c)	All metals are easily corroded.	☐	☐
d)	Malleable metals can be hammered into different shapes.	☐	☐
e)	Metals with high strength are good for holding weight.	☐	☐

Q2 For his science homework Joshua comes up with a list of metals used around his **house**. Draw lines to match up the metals with their uses. Some metals have more than one use.

Metal: Lead, Aluminium, Copper, Iron/Steel

Uses: to make fixings, water pipes, electrical wires, window frames, supporting structures, flashing on chimneys

Metal is often found on roofs, flashing around chimneys.

Q3 Malcolm is a **builder**. The different projects he works on use different materials with different **properties**. Use words from the list below to complete the paragraph about the properties of different **metals**. Only use each word once.

copper   lead   rust   strength

Some metals have great .... , which makes them ideal for support structures like roof beams. For some purposes it is important to use a metal that is soft and malleable, e.g. .... All metals conduct electricity, but .... is a really good conductor so it's often used for electrical wiring. Iron and steel are cheap but they will .... if they are not protected.

Section 2.2 — My Home

Metals

Q4 Heather works in a **builders' shop**. They sell various metals in different sizes, shapes and lengths. The table shows five of the materials available and some of their **properties**.

Metal	Melting point (°C)	Malleability	Resistance to corrosion	Strength	Other comments
Steel	1430	Poor	Poor	Excellent	Very cheap
Aluminium	660	Poor	Excellent	Good	—
Iron	1538	Good	Poor	Excellent	Cheap
Lead	327	Excellent	Good	Poor	Dull, grey colour, toxic
Copper	1085	Good	Excellent	Average	Excellent conductor

Use the information in the table to answer the following questions.

a) One customer comes into the shop and asks for some **steel** to make a new **window frame**. Give **one** reason why steel would **not** be a good choice of material to make window frames.

....

b) The shop used to sell lots of **lead** but sales have fallen over the years.

i) Give **one** reason why we don't use lead to make fittings such as door handles and taps.

....

ii) Most **water pipes** used to be made from lead.
Suggest **two** reasons why lead was thought to be a good metal for this use.

1. ....

2. ....

iii) Today most water pipes are made from **copper**.
Suggest **one** reason why it is better to make water pipes from copper than lead.

....

c) The builders' merchants supply **aluminium** to a company that produces small wind turbines that can be attached to a roof to generate electricity. Give **two** reasons why aluminium is a good choice of material for this use.

1. ....

2. ....

d) Heather suggests some **iron sheeting** for a customer's roof.
Suggest **one** reason why this is not a good idea.

....

Section 2.2 — My Home

Polymers

Q1 Gareth is a builder. He uses the polymer **polyethene** as a building material.

a) Where do the chemicals used to make polymers come from?

....

b) Tick the box next to the **true** statement below.

The monomer of polyethene is ethene. ☐

The polymer of polyethene is ethane. ☐

The monomer of polyethene is ethane. ☐

c) Other then polyethene, name two polymers used in the construction industry.

1. ....

2. ....

Q2 **Polymers** have many **uses** in the modern world. Complete the passage about polymers and some of their uses using words from the box.

electricity   heat   shopping bags   poor   insulators

Some polymers, e.g. polyethene, are very flexible. This property makes them good for .... and squeezy bottles. Most polymers are .... conductors of .... and .... Because polymers are good .... they're often used to make casings for electrical appliances.

Q3 A **designer** is looking at different polymers that could be used to make a new range of **chairs**.

Polymer	Flexibility
Polyethene	Very flexible
Polypropene	Not flexible, very rigid
PVC	Stretchy and rigid

a) Explain why the designer would not want to make chairs out of polyethene.

....

b) Which polymer should the designer pick? Explain your choice.

....

Section 2.2 — My Home

Polymers

Q4 Peter works in a factory that makes **plastic bottles**.

The polymer the factory uses has a **low melting point**.
Suggest why this polymer is suitable for making plastic bottles.

....

....

Q5 Gladys sees an advert for a **frying pan** in a magazine.
The pan's handle is made from a **polymer**.

a) Suggest **one** advantage of making the handle of a frying pan from a polymer.

....

....

b) Suggest one reason why the base of the frying pan is **not** made from a polymer.

....

Q6 Felicity is a **material scientist** working for a company that produces a range of kitchen appliances and tools. Complete the table by describing one **property** that the polymer used to make each object would need to have.

Use of polymer	Property the polymer would need
Spatula	
Work surface	
Kettle casing	
Insulation around the kettle's electrical lead	

Q7 Barry has designed a new household cleaner which kills 99.99% of known bacteria. He has decided to use a polymer to make the **bottle**.

Suggest three **properties** that this polymer will need.

1. ....

2. ....

3. ....

Section 2.2 — My Home

Ceramics

Q1 Walter is a salesman in a bathroom store.
He suggests a new **ceramic bathroom** to some customers.

a) Give **two** properties of ceramics that make them suitable for use in bathrooms.

1. ....

2. ....

b) Give **one** problem with using ceramics for bathroom fittings.

....

c) Suggest why some customers may still prefer ceramic to metal.

....

Q2 Andy runs a bakery. He decides to buy a new large oven for baking the bread.

a) Give one reason why ceramics are suitable for lining an oven.

....

....

b) A glass window is smashed at the bakery. Glass is a type of ceramic.
Suggest one property of glass that makes it bad for making windows.

....

Q3 Ceramics are used for a number of **fixtures and fittings** around the home.
Put ticks in the boxes below to show why the objects listed are made from ceramics.

You can tick more than one box for each object.

	Hard wearing — it doesn't scratch easily	Waterproof and smooth — it's easily cleaned and hygienic	High melting point — it's fire resistant	Inert — it doesn't corrode
Porcelain toilet				
Ceramic kitchen sink				
Brick fire place				
Glass coffee table				

Top Tips: Ceramics are used for loads of different things and for good reason too — they're hard-wearing, waterproof, inert, have a high melting point and they're available in a whole range of pretty patterns and colours. The big downside is that they're brittle — they break fairly easily.

Section 2.2 — My Home

Composites

Q1 Majid has written a report about **composites**. Use the words below to complete the paragraph.

> wood   furniture   construction   strength   metal   composites   combination

.... are used by manufacturers as they can't always find one material with the properties they need. Mixing two materials produces a new material with a .... of the properties of the materials it's made from. MDF is a composite made up of bits of .... stuck together. MDF is strong and it's used a lot in .... Reinforced concrete adds rods of .... to concrete which gives the material .... It's used a lot in ....

Q2 SGT Plastics produce **fibreglass**. Fibreglass is a material made of **plastic** reinforced with small fibres of **glass**.

a) Give one advantage of using fibreglass over ordinary plastic.

....

....

....

b) The table shows how the strength of fibreglass changes with the percentage of glass in the mixture.

Percentage glass	Tensile strength (MPa)
20	130
40	160
60	205
80	245

MPa is short for megapascal — a unit of strength.

i) Plot the data on the grid.

ii) Describe how the percentage of glass affects the tensile strength.

....

....

Section 2.2 — My Home

Choosing Materials for a Product

Q1 Springsteen Building Supplies provide **four** types of **material** for the construction industry.

a) The table shows the annual percentage sales of materials from Springsteen's.
Complete the table by calculating the annual percentage sales for iron.

Material	% of annual sales
Composites	22
Timber	33
Iron	
Steel	26

b) Give one **advantage** of using timber rather than iron or steel as a building material.

....

c) Give one **disadvantage** of using timber rather than iron or steel as a building material.

....

d) Some people in the industry predict that the amount of timber sold is likely to increase. Suggest a possible reason for this.

Metal isn't a sustainable resource.

....

....

Q2 Tony decides to build a **slide** for his garden.
He starts by considering the possible materials he could use.

a) List two **properties** that the material for the slide would need to have.

1. ....

2. ....

b) Circle the best material from the list below that Tony could use for the slide.

a polymer   glass   cement

c) Give one reason why each of the following would **not** be suitable for the slide.

i) Iron ....

....

ii) Ceramics ....

....

Section 2.2 — My Home

Choosing Materials for a Product

Q3 Anna has just bought an old house that was built in 1672. Unfortunately over the years it has become a bit run down. Anna's about to begin **rebuilding** it.

Because the building is so old she must use **traditional** alternatives to **modern** building materials.

a) The **window frames** need replacing. Anna cannot install plastic window frames. She must use wooden ones instead.

   i) What are the advantages of using wood instead of plastic? Circle the correct answer(s).

   it's flammable   it's a traditional material so it suits the age of the house   it's waterproof   it's sustainable

   ii) What are the advantages of using plastic instead of wood? Circle the correct answer(s).

   it lasts longer   it can be painted any colour   it's resistant to corrosion   it doesn't react with the glass like wood does

b) One of the **support beams** needs replacing. Anna wanted to use steel but has been told that she must use wood. Give **one advantage** of using steel instead of wood for the beam.

....

....

c) Anna can choose to use either modern **fibreglass** insulation or traditional **straw bale** insulation.

   i) Give two reasons why it may be better for Anna to use straw bale insulation.

   1. ....

   2. ....

   ii) Briefly describe two **problems** Anna may face if she chooses straw bale insulation.

   1. ....

   2. ....

d) Anna wants to build a new garage. She can't decide whether to choose **brick** or **cob walls**. Tick the correct box to show if the following statements are true or false.

	True	False
i) Cob is made up of sand, limestone and water.	☐	☐
ii) Brick walls are much stronger than cob walls.	☐	☐
iii) It's cheaper to build a cob wall than a brick wall.	☐	☐
iv) Brick walls are better for the environment than cob walls.	☐	☐

Section 2.2 — My Home

Choosing Materials for a Product

Q4 Ken is building a **garage** on the side of his house.
He has drawn up the following list of what the garage must have.

- Strong and sturdy walls.
- Solid foundations.
- A waterproof and secure roof.
- Windows for workshop area at the rear.
- Secure entrance.

a) Ken is thinking about the material for the roof.

  i) Suggest a suitable material Ken could use for the **roof**.

  ....

  ii) Give one reason to explain your choice.

  ....

b) Give one advantage of using **bricks** to build the **walls** of the garage.

....

c) To ensure the garage is secure Ken decided to use **fibreglass** for the **windows**.
Give one advantage of using fibreglass instead of ordinary glass.

....

d) Ken is using **reinforced concrete** in the structure of the garage.

  i) Reinforced concrete is a composite. Give two disadvantages of composites.

  1. ....

  2. ....

  ii) Give one reason why reinforced concrete is a **good** choice for the structure of the garage.

  ....

Top Tips: As you may well have guessed, these pages were all about being able to select the right materials for a job. Make sure you know about modern building materials and their advantages and disadvantages compared to traditional materials, like good old timber frames and cob walls.

Section 2.2 — My Home

Fuels from Crude Oil

Q1 Trevor works on an **oil rig** in the North Sea, where they extract crude oil. Tick the boxes to show whether the following statements about crude oil are **true** or **false**.

    True False

a) Crude oil is a fossil fuel.

b) Diesel is used as a fuel in cars, buses and trains.

c) Heating oil from crude oil is used as fuel in aeroplanes.

d) All fuels have the same energy content.

e) Natural gas comes from crude oil.

True or false — crude oil makes a tasty salad dressing?

Q2 Crude oil contains a mixture of different **hydrocarbons**. These are **separated** to produce fuels like **petrol** and **diesel**.

a) What is a hydrocarbon?

....

b) Circle **all** of the compounds below that are hydrocarbons.

CO_2 C_3H_8 C_2H_4 CO H_2O C_2H_5OH

c) Most of the hydrocarbon molecules in crude oil have the general formula C_nH_{2n+2}. Work out the formula of a hydrocarbon with **12** carbon atoms.

....

....

Q3 When diesel is burnt in a car engine, **energy** is released to power the car.

a) Diesel is a hydrocarbon. Fill in the blanks to complete the word equation for the combustion of a hydrocarbon.

    hydrocarbon + ... → .... + ...

b) Circle the correct answer to complete the following sentences:

   i) The larger the hydrocarbon molecule, the **more / less** oxygen is needed for combustion

   ii) Smaller hydrocarbon molecules produce **greater / smaller** amounts of carbon dioxide and water during combustion than larger ones.

Higher only

c) Complete the balanced symbol equation for the combustion of the hydrocarbon shown.

    C_7H_{16} + ... O_2 → .... CO_2 + ... H_2O (+ energy)

Section 2.2 — My Home

Problems with Fuels from Crude Oil

Q1 Fill in the gaps using the words below to complete the passage.

> electricity   cars   atmosphere
> renewable   non-renewable   wind power

Power stations burn huge amounts of fossil fuels to make ....
Fossil fuels are also used to power .... Burning fossil fuels from
crude oil releases gases which pollute the .... Crude oil is a
.... fuel — there's only a finite amount. This has forced scientists to
develop .... energy sources, for example, ...

Q2 Anita is a scientist who measures pollution in the **atmosphere**.

a) Anita is asked to produce a graph to show how the **carbon dioxide** (CO_2) concentration in the atmosphere has changed over the last few hundred years.

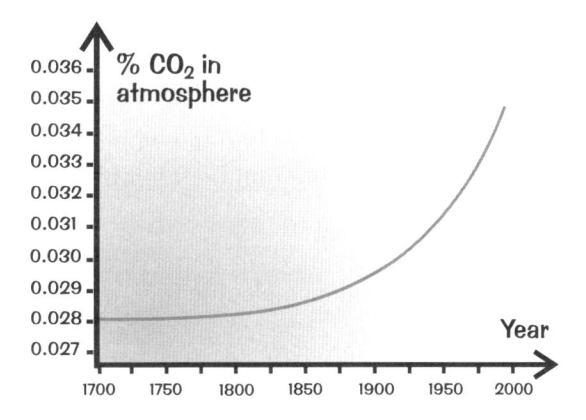

i) Describe the **trend** shown by the graph.

....

ii) Give the main **cause** of this trend.

....

iii) Describe the effect the trend shown in the graph is having on the Earth's **average temperature**.

....

iv) Give the **name** of this effect.

....

b) Other than carbon dioxide, name one gas that pollutes the atmosphere.

....

Section 2.2 — My Home

Alternatives to Fossil Fuels

Q1 Look at the list of **energy resources** below.

nuclear   wave   coal   hydroelectric   solar   gas   tidal   oil   wind

a) Circle the resources on the list that are **renewable**.

b) Which two energy resources in the list involve seawater?

1. ....   2. ....

Q2 **Waves can be used to drive a generator, which produces electricity.**

a) What are the **advantages** of wave power? Circle the **two** correct answers.

no pollution   very reliable   low set up costs   no fuel costs

b) What are the **disadvantages** of wave power? Circle the **two** correct answers.

high pollution   high set-up costs   unreliable   high running costs

Q3 There are plans to build a large **tidal barrage** on an estuary in Scotland. Kevin has written a report about the possible effects of this on the surrounding **environment**.

a) The following statements explain how a tidal barrage works but they are in the wrong order. Put them in the correct order by writing the numbers 1-5 in the boxes.

The tide comes in and fills up the estuary. ☐

The turbines drive a generator that produces electricity. ☐

The water turns turbines as it passes through. ☐

As the tide goes out, it passes back through the barrage. ☐

The tide is held back by the barrage. ☐

b) Building the barrage would flood a large area surrounding the estuary. Describe how this might affect the **wildlife** in the area.

....

c) Apart from the effects on wildlife, give one other possible **disadvantage** of building the barrage.

....

d) i) Give one reason why tidal power is **reliable**.

....

ii) Give one reason why the **amount** of energy provided by tidal power can vary.

....

Section 2.2 — My Home

Alternatives to Fossil Fuels

Q4 A coal-fired power station in Scotland is going to be replaced by **wind turbines**. There are three possible sites. **Site A** has an average wind speed of **8 m/s**, **Site B** has an average wind speed of **9 m/s**, and **Site C** has an average wind speed of **11 m/s**.

a) Which site would produce the most electricity? ....

b) Site C is near the coast in the sea. What are the benefits of placing the wind turbines at Site C? Tick **two** boxes from the list below.

It is less likely people will complain about the noise. ☐

They're less likely to get damaged. ☐

It doesn't matter if you pollute the sea. ☐

There is generally more wind around the coast. ☐

c) Give two **disadvantages** of installing wind turbines.

1. ....

2. ....

Q5 Answer the following questions by putting a circle around the correct answer.

a) Which power source can have a large impact on the environment through flooding?

    wind   **solar**   **hydroelectric**   **nuclear**

b) Which power source can make electricity whenever its needed?

    wind   **solar**   **hydroelectric**   **tidal**

c) Which power source does not pollute the environment once built?

    wind   **solar**   **hydroelectric**   **all three**

Q6 Karen lives in a hot sunny area. She is considering buying **solar panels** for the roof of her house.

a) Explain how fitting the solar panels would be good for the environment.

....

....

b) Suggest why solar panels would be a good choice for Karen.

....

....

c) Give one **disadvantage** of using solar panels.

....

Section 2.2 — My Home

Alternatives to Fossil Fuels

Q7 Explain why:

a) geothermal energy can only be used in very few places.

....

b) biomass is a 'renewable' source of energy.

....

Q8 Mr Saleem is a cattle farmer in India. He has decided to use biomass to produce electricity.

a) Name the source of waste Mr Saleem is likely to use.

....

b) Describe how biomass is used to produce electricity in power stations.

....

Q9 Tick the correct boxes to show whether these statements apply to generating electricity from **geothermal** energy or **biomass**.

	Biomass	Geothermal
a) Set-up costs are low.	☐	☐
b) Does not release CO_2.	☐	☐
c) Possible in any country in the world.	☐	☐
d) Reduces the need for landfill sites.	☐	☐

Darling, I think we need more poo...

Q10 Fiza and Julie are discussing the environmental impacts of using biomass to generate electricity.

Fiza says: **"Burning organic waste gives off harmful gases."**

Julie says: **"But it's better than just burying the waste and burning fossil fuels instead."**

Who do you think is right? Explain your answer.

....

....

Top Tips: Burning animal poo is nothing new — people have been doing it for years, and many still do. For instance, if you're a nomadic yak herder in Mongolia, you probably don't have mains electricity, but you do have lots of yak poo. Dry it, burn it, and you'll have a nice warm tent.

Section 2.2 — My Home

Alternatives to Fossil Fuels

Q11 Nuclear power could be used to help meet our future energy needs. Circle the correct word from each pair in the paragraph below to explain how **nuclear power** works.

> Nuclear power is a **renewable** / **non-renewable** energy resource. It involves splitting atoms by a process called nuclear **fission** / **fusion**. This releases large amounts of heat energy from small amounts of **neon** / **uranium**. The energy produced is used to heat **oil** / **water**, to turn it into steam. The steam drives a turbine, which in turn drives a generator, which produces **fuel** / **electricity**.

Q12 Homer works as a safety officer at a nuclear power plant. He is responsible for getting rid of nuclear waste **safely**.

Tick the box to show whether these statements are true or false.

	True	False
a) Nuclear waste is radioactive.	☐	☐
b) Over time, nuclear waste becomes less dangerous.	☐	☐
c) Nuclear waste can be used as fuel for cars.	☐	☐

Q13 The table below shows the amount of **carbon dioxide** produced by different fuels.

Fuel	Amount of carbon dioxide (tonnes) produced by 1 tonne of fuel
Coal	2.0
Oil	2.5
Gas	2.5
Uranium	0

a) i) State which fuel, in the table above, does **not** produce any carbon dioxide.

....

ii) Explain why this is a **benefit** for the environment.

....

b) Bob thinks that uranium is the best **long-term** solution for producing power. Suggest why he thinks this.

....

....

Section 2.2 — My Home

Comparing Energy Resources

Q1 Claire works for an energy company. She is responsible for choosing which **energy resource** to use in different places.

List **three** factors that Claire should consider when deciding on an energy resource.

1. ....

2. ....

3. ....

Q2 The map below shows a small island. Five sites are labelled A - E. These sites have been picked for **energy developments**. Scientists are looking at the potential of each site.

a) Which site would be most suitable for a **tidal barrage**? Explain why.

....

b) Which site would be most suitable for a **hydroelectric power station**? Explain why.

....

c) Which two sites would be most suitable for a **wind farm**? Explain why.

....

....

d) Sites D and E are both being considered as the location for a **wave power station**. Which of these two sites would you recommend? Explain your answer.

....

....

Section 2.2 — My Home

Generating Electricity

Q1 The diagram below shows a **power station**.

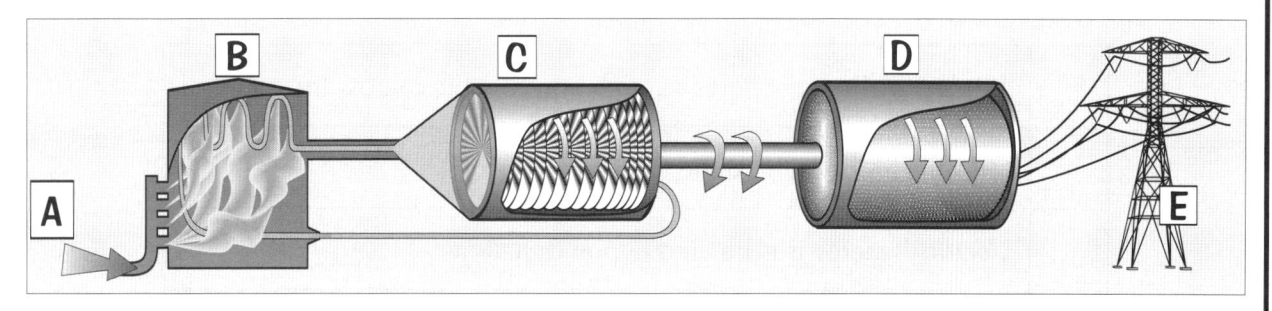

a) Draw lines to match up the parts of the diagram with the correct steps.

A — Steam is used to turn a turbine.

B — The electricity is delivered via a network of cables.

C — The fuel is burnt and the heat energy is used to boil water.

D — Fuel (e.g. coal, oil, or gas) enters the boiler.

E — The turbine rotates a generator to create electricity.

b) Give the name of the piece of equipment that is used instead of a boiler in a **nuclear** power station to generate heat.

....

c) i) Explain what is meant by the term '**National Grid**'.

....

....

ii) Albert and June live **a long way** away from a power station. Briefly explain why the National Grid is good for them.

....

....

....

Section 2.2 — My Home

Supplying Electricity

Q1 Number these statements 1 to 5 to show the order of the steps that are needed to deliver energy to Mrs Miggins' house so that she can boil the kettle.

	An electrical current flows through power cables across the country.
	Mrs Miggins boils the kettle for tea.
	Electrical energy is generated in power stations
	The voltage of the supply is raised.
	The voltage of the supply is reduced.

Q2 Circle the correct word in each pair to complete the sentences below.

a) The National Grid transmits energy at **high / low** voltage and **high / low** current.

b) A **step-up / step-down** transformer is used to **increase / decrease** the voltage of the supply before electricity is transmitted.

c) Using a low **current / voltage** makes sure there is not much energy wasted.

d) A **step-up / step-down** transformer is used to reduce the voltage of the electricity.

e) At a **high / low** voltage, electricity can be used safely in homes.

f) Electrical pylons **need / do not need** insulators to carry electricity safely.

Q3 Laura is looking for a new house. She looks at a house which has **power cables** running over the end of the garden.

Give two reasons why Laura might have **concerns** about living so close to the power lines.

1. ....

....

2. ....

....

Top Tips: Power at the flick of a switch is a pretty awesome idea if you think about it. The National Grid is great for getting electricity around the country quickly. But don't forget that transporting so much of the stuff can cause problems for the environment.

Section 2.2 — My Home

Calculating Power and Current

Q1 Use the words below to fill in the gaps in the equation.

| current | power |

.... = potential difference × ....

Q2 Martin wants to know what the **electrical information** on the sticker on the back of his computer means. The information shows values with different units.

Draw lines to match the electrical terms to their correct units.

Potential difference   Amps (A)

Current   Watts (W)

Power   Volts (V)

Q3 Robert has a number of **electrical appliances** and is not sure of their **power**. He tests each of the appliances. He designs a table to record the results in **amps**, **watts** and **volts**.

Just use the formula for power.

Complete the table by calculating the power of each component.

Component	Potential Difference	Current	Power
Microphone	12	1	
Lamp	12	2	
Buzzer	230	0.6	
Motor	230	3.2	

Section 2.3 — My Property

Calculating Energy Use and Costs

Q1 Clara is trying to reduce the amount of **electricity** she uses. Below are the **powers** of the **household appliances** she uses most often.

Number the appliances in order of how much they would **cost** if they were all left on for the **same amount of time**. Make **1** the most expensive, and **6** the cheapest.

- ☐ Kettle 2.4 kW
- ☐ Mobile phone charger 4.8 W
- ☐ Table lamp 60 W
- ☐ Hairdryer 1200 W
- ☐ Hair straighteners 170 W
- ☐ Electric shower 7.5 kW

Q2 Using the formula **power = energy transferred ÷ time**, calculate the **power** of these **appliances**:

a) A **radio** that transfers 40 J of energy to heat and sound energy in 2 seconds.

....

....

Don't forget that energy is in joules and time is in seconds.

b) An **electric blender** that transfers 18 kJ of energy to kinetic, heat and sound energy in 1 minute.

....

....

c) A **toaster** that transfers 153 kJ of energy to heat energy in 90 seconds.

....

....

Q3 Richard thinks that he is using too much **electricity** in his home and that his electricity bill will be very **expensive**. He draws a table to help him work out if he is right.

Appliance	Power (kW)	Time left on (hours)	Energy used (kWh)	Cost (p)
Electric heater	2	3	6	120
Travel iron	1.2	0.5		
Surround sound hi-fi	0.5	1.5		
Light bulb	0.06	5		

a) Calculate the electrical **energy used** by each appliance and write your answers in the table. The first one has been done for you.

b) The Wattless Electricity Company charges **20p per kWh**. Complete the table by calculating how much each appliance costs to run for the time given. The first one has been done for you.

Section 2.3 — My Property

Calculating Energy Use and Costs

Q4 The last time Anthony read his **electricity meter**, it read **6582 kWh**.
The diagram below shows what his meter reads now.

`0 0 0 9 8 1 4 | 5 |`

The last number shows tenths of a kWh.

a) Calculate how much electricity Anthony has used since he last checked his meter.

....

b) Anthony's electricity supplier charges **11p per kWh**.
Calculate how much Anthony has spent on electricity since he last read his meter.

....

Q5 Mr Havel recently received his **electricity bill**. Unfortunately, he tore off the bottom part to write a shopping list.

a) Work out how many **kWh** of energy Mr Havel used in the three months from June to September.

....

Customer: Havel, V

Date: Meter Reading:

11 / 06 / 10   34259 kWh
10 / 09 / 10   34783 kWh

Total Cost @ 9.7p per kWh

b) Calculate Mr Havel's bill for the three months to the nearest penny.

....

....

Q6 Tina's mum tells her off for leaving a 0.06 kW lamp on overnight — about 9 hours every night.
Tina says her mum uses **more energy** by using an 8 kW shower for 0.25 hours every day.

Is Tina right? Calculate how much energy each person uses and compare your results.

....

....

....

....

Top Tips: Although there's quite a bit of maths on these pages, it's nothing too difficult. There are two formulas you need to be able to use — one to work out power and one to calculate cost.

Section 2.3 — My Property

Efficiency

Q1 Kaitlin is shopping for a new **fridge** and is keen to buy an **efficient** one.

Fill in the gaps in the following passage about efficiency using words from the box.

| | efficient | | sound | | better | | wasted | |
| used | | heat | | converting | | useful | | energy |

Electrical appliances convert .... energy .... from one form to another. All of the input energy is electrical but not all of this is converted into .... useful .... energy. Some of the energy is .... wasted .... This energy does not disappear — it is still there but in forms which can't be easily .... used .... Energy is often wasted as .... heat .... or .... sound .... energy. The .... better .... an appliance is at .... converting .... the input energy into useful energy, the more .... efficient .... it is said to be.

Q2 For a school project, Ash is given the **input** and **output** energies for some household appliances. For each appliance, circle the **useful** energy output(s), and calculate the appliance's **efficiency**.

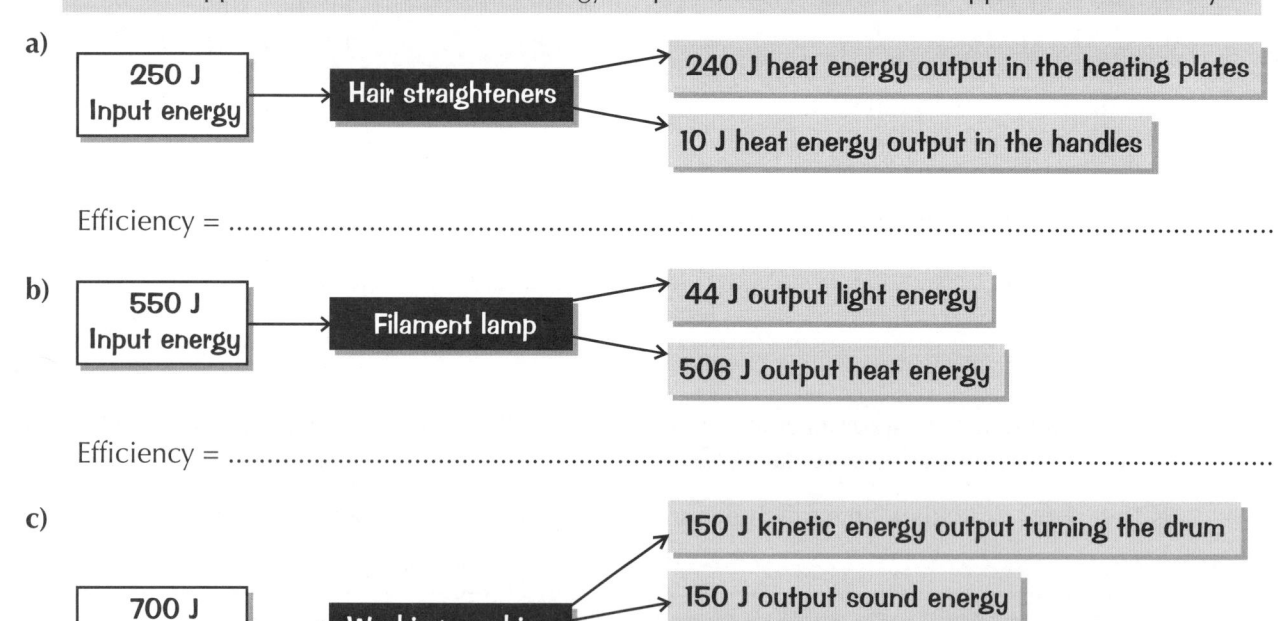

a) 250 J Input energy → Hair straighteners →
- 240 J heat energy output in the heating plates
- 10 J heat energy output in the handles

Efficiency = ...

b) 550 J Input energy → Filament lamp →
- 44 J output light energy
- 506 J output heat energy

Efficiency = ...

c) 700 J Input energy → Washing machine →
- 150 J kinetic energy output turning the drum
- 150 J output sound energy
- 300 J heat energy output in the water
- 100 J heat energy output in the body of the machine

Efficiency = ...

Top Tips: Efficiency is one of those rare topics in physics that makes sense — if you put loads of energy into a machine, but get little useful energy out in return, your machine isn't efficient. Easy.

Section 2.3 — My Property

Energy Labels

Q1 Bill's deciding whether or not to buy an old 'Chillomax' fridge-freezer or a brand new 'Icebreeze' one. Luke checks the **EU energy labels** for the different machines to help him choose.

a) Explain why EU energy labels are useful.

....

....

The energy labels for the two fridge-freezers are shown below:

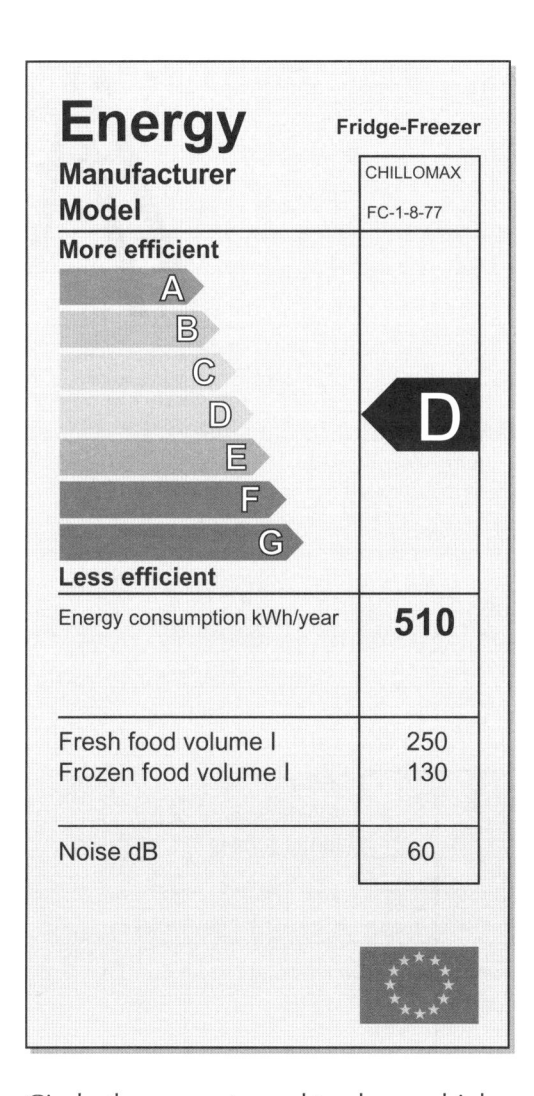

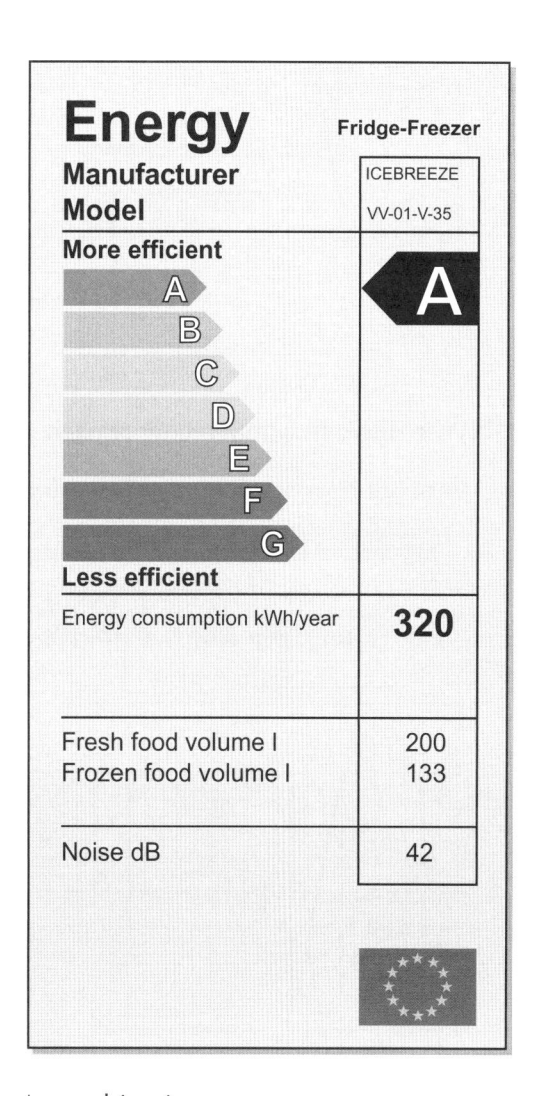

Energy Fridge-Freezer	
Manufacturer	CHILLOMAX
Model	FC-1-8-77
More efficient — A, B, C, **D**, E, F, G — Less efficient	
Energy consumption kWh/year	**510**
Fresh food volume l	250
Frozen food volume l	130
Noise dB	60

Energy Fridge-Freezer	
Manufacturer	ICEBREEZE
Model	VV-01-V-35
More efficient — **A**, B, C, D, E, F, G — Less efficient	
Energy consumption kWh/year	**320**
Fresh food volume l	200
Frozen food volume l	133
Noise dB	42

b) Circle the correct word to show which manufacturer's machine is:

   i) the most energy efficient.   **Chillomax   Icebreeze**

   ii) able to store the largest volume of frozen food?   **Chillomax   Icebreeze**

c) Give one advantage of the Chillomax fridge-freezer over the Icebreeze model.

....

d) Which manufacturer's machine would be the cheapest to run?   ....

Section 2.3 — My Property

Sankey Diagrams

Q1 This diagram shows the energy changes in a **lightbulb**. The diagram is drawn to scale.

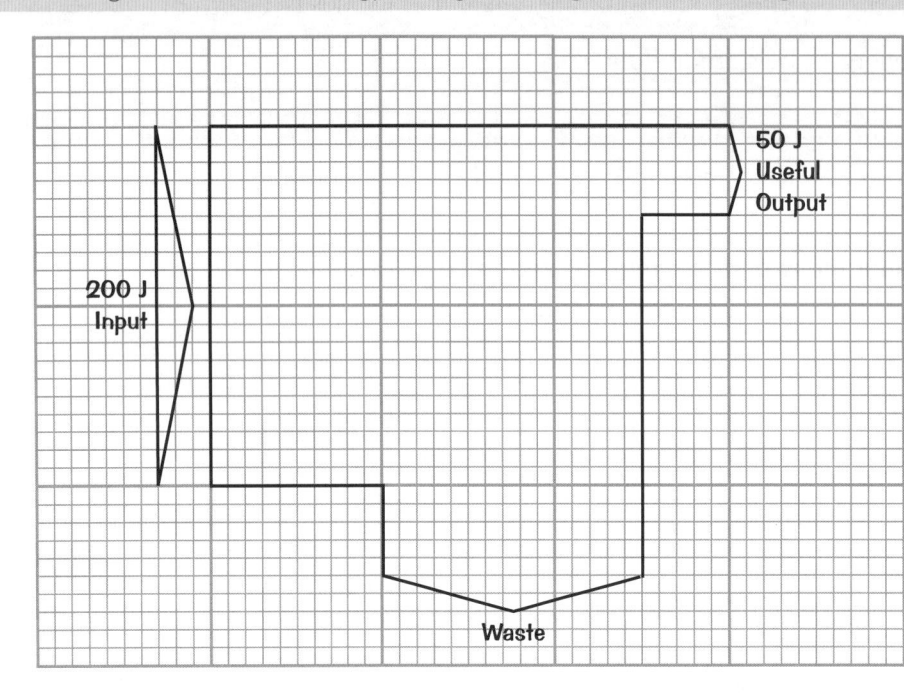

a) Write down how much energy each **small square** is worth. .... J

b) Work out how much energy is **wasted**. .... J

Q2 The Sankey diagram below is for a **washing machine**. The machine works by turning a drum that contains dirty clothes, hot water and washing powder.

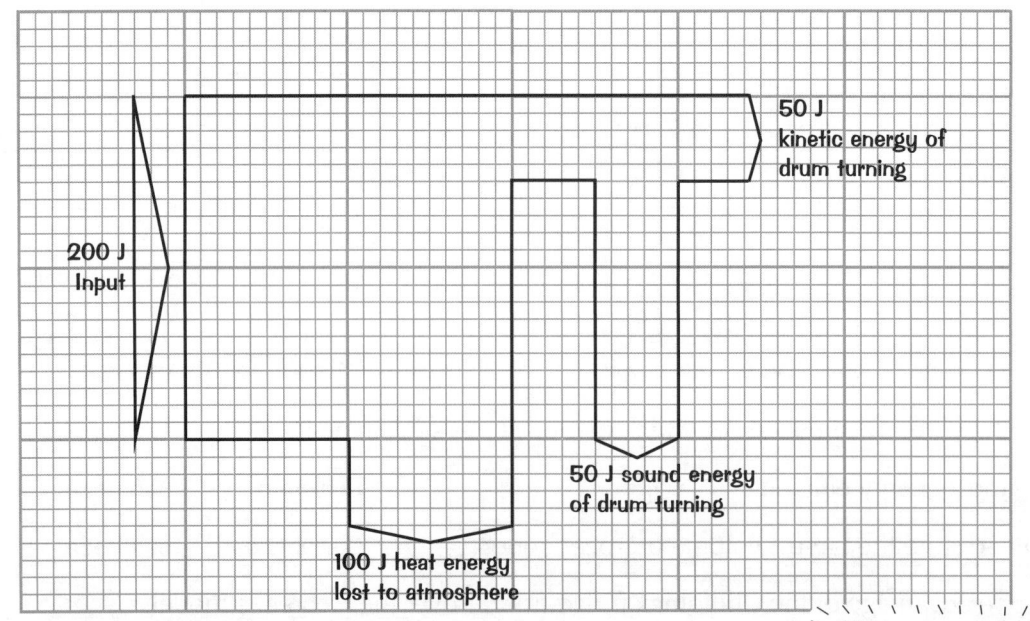

$$\text{efficiency} = \frac{\text{useful energy}}{\text{total energy}} \times 100$$

a) Write down the total amount of energy **wasted**. .... J

b) Work out the **efficiency** of the washing machine. Give your answer as a percentage.

....

Section 2.3 — My Property

Electromagnetic Waves

Q1 Steven is doing his homework on **electromagnetic radiation**.

What can Steven say about the electromagnetic radiation being given out by a light bulb? Complete the sentence by circling the correct word in each pair.

> Electromagnetic radiation travels as waves and moves energy / matter from one place to another without moving any energy / matter.

Q2 Jimmy is making a list of all the types of **electromagnetic waves** he can think of.

a) Circle the two types of wave that should **not** be on his list.

radio waves   gamma rays   seismic waves   visible light   X-rays

microwaves   infrared   water waves   ultra violet

b) Add the other seven waves into the boxes below in order of increasing frequency.

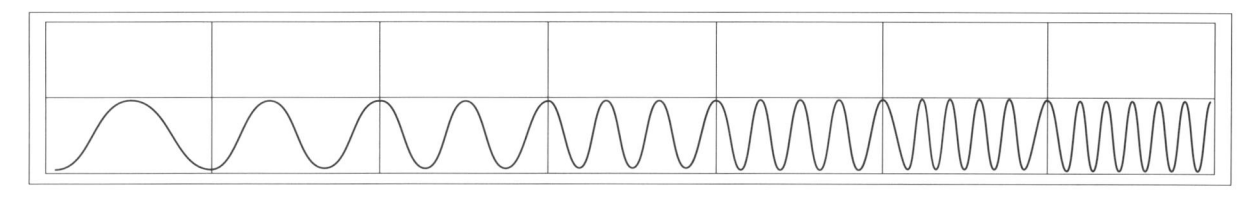

c) Give the type of EM wave that has the **shortest wavelength**? ....

d) Give the type of EM wave that has the **lowest frequency**? ....

Q3 All waves have a **frequency** and a **wavelength**.

a) Circle the sentence that is true for a wave with a frequency of **25 hertz**.

There are 25 waves per second.   There is one wave every 25 seconds.

b) Describe what happens to the frequency of a wave as its wavelength increases.

....

c) The diagram shows a waveform.

Which of A, B or C is the length of one whole wave? Write the letter below.

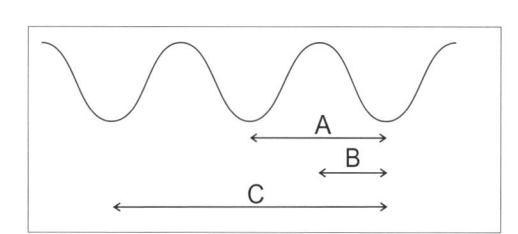

....

Section 2.3 — My Property

The Wave Equation

Q1 A rugby player jumps into a canal, sending waves across to the other side. A wave arrives **once every second**. The distance between their peaks is **0.2 m**.

velocity = frequency × wavelength

a) Write down the **frequency** of the waves. ....

b) Use the **wave equation** to calculate the **velocity** of the waves.

....

Q2 The graph shows a **sound wave**.

a) How many **complete** vibrations are shown?

....

b) **How long** does it take to make each vibration?

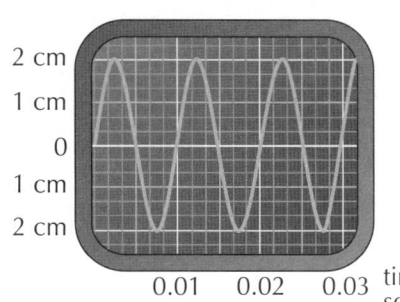

....

Q3 A ripple in a pond travels at **0.5 m/s**. It makes a duck bob up and down **twice every second**.

a) Give the **frequency** of the duck's bobbing. ....

b) When the duck is on the crest of a wave, work out **how far away** the next crest is.

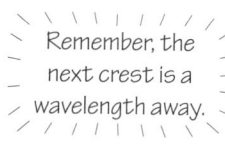

....

....

Remember, the next crest is a wavelength away.

Higher only

Q4 **Green light** travels at 3×10^8 m/s and has a wavelength of about 5×10^{-7} m.

Calculate the **frequency** of green light. Give the correct unit in your answer.

....

....

Higher only

Q5 Put the following frequencies in order of **size**, from the **highest** frequency to the **lowest** frequency.

90 MHz   900 kHz   9 000 000 Hz 9×10^4 Hz 9×10^2 MHz

It'll help if you put them all into hertz, and in standard form.

....

Section 2.3 — My Property

Uses of Radio Waves and Microwaves

Q1 Henry's radio works by picking up radio waves. As the radio waves meet objects they can either be transmitted, reflected or absorbed.

a) Draw lines to match each of the words below to its correct explanation.

Transmitted — the waves bounce back, like light off a mirror

Reflected — the wave's energy is transferred to the substance, like microwaves heating food

Absorbed — the waves pass through the substance, like light through glass

b) Explain why low frequency waves, like radio waves, are better for long distance communication than high frequency waves.

....

....

Q2 Karl is studying **radio waves** of different **wavelengths**.
Complete the passage to describe how different radio waves are transmitted.

reflected   longest   shortest   electromagnetic   wavelengths

There's a range of .... within the radio part of the .... spectrum. The .... radio waves are transmitted directly to a receiver. Radio waves with medium wavelengths are .... off the atmosphere. The .... radio waves are able to bend around the earth.

Q3 Sarah uses her microwave oven to heat a beef and onion pie.

a) Other than microwave ovens, name two technologies that use microwaves.

1. ....

2. ....

b) Explain how microwave ovens are able to heat food.

....

....

Section 2.3 — My Property

Uses of Infrared, Ultraviolet and Visible Light

Q1 Julia is testing the **remote controls** for her TV set and DVD player. Remote controls work by sending a beam of **infrared waves** to the TV or other device.

a) Explain how you can tell that the remote controls do **not** use **visible light**?

....

b) Use statements A-C to answer the following questions.

> A — Infrared waves can be transmitted through glass.
> B — Infrared waves cannot pass through any solid object.
> C — Infrared waves cannot pass through opaque solid objects.

Opaque means the opposite of transparent. An opaque object is something you can't see through.

i) Julia's DVD machine is in a cabinet with a glass door. She finds she can use the DVD remote even when this door is closed. What does this tell her about infrared waves? ....

ii) Julia notices that if a magazine is placed in front of the receptor on the base of the TV then the TV remote cannot be used. The same happens if furniture or people block the path of the beam. What does this tell her about infrared waves? ....

Q2 Bill is fitting Sid's house with a broadband internet connection. Broadband internet uses **optical fibres**.

a) Name a type of electromagnetic wave that is usually carried by an optical fibre.

....

b) Describe how a signal travels along an optical fibre.

....

....

c) i) Once he's got his broadband fitted, Sid starts researching sun tanning beds online. Name the type of electromagnetic radiation that's used in sun tanning beds.

....

ii) Explain why this type of radiation is used in sun tanning beds.

....

Top Tips: You need to make sure you know about the properties and uses of every part of the electromagnetic spectrum. There are also some risks that you need to know about. Meet page 83...

Section 2.3 — My Property

Dangers of Electromagnetic Radiation

Q1 Michael has injured his knee playing **football**. His coach takes him to the hospital for an **X-ray** of the injury. Complete the passage by filling in the gaps with the words below.

dangerous   gamma   lead   reduce   radiographers   screens

X-rays and .... rays aren't used in the home because they're too

.... Specialists like ...., who need to use

X-rays for their work, must protect themselves. Radiographers wear ....

aprons and stand behind lead .... in order to

.... the risk of damaging themselves.

Q2 Kate is running a training course for hospital staff on possible **dangers** from X-rays, gamma rays, infrared, and ultraviolet rays.

She makes a table to show the risks from these four types of electromagnetic radiation.

Type of EM radiation	Risk
Infrared light	
Ultraviolet	
X-rays	
Gamma rays	

a) Put the following statements into the correct boxes in the table.

Risk of cancer within the body.   **Risk of skin cancer.**   **Risk of burns or heatstroke.**

b) Label each end of the arrow with the words "most dangerous" and "least dangerous" to show the order of risk.

Q3 Explain why **high frequency** waves like gamma rays are generally more **dangerous** than low frequency waves like radio waves. Talk about **energy** in your answer.

....

....

....

Section 2.3 — My Property

Mixed Questions for Sections 2.1-2.3

Q1 Ryan has **diabetes**. The specialist at his hospital is explaining the role of **insulin** in the body.

a) Circle the correct words to explain how **insulin** works to **reduce** blood sugar levels in the body.

> When blood sugar levels are **high** / **low** insulin is released by the
> **pancreas** / **liver**. The liver **adds** / **removes** glucose from the **blood** / **urine**.
> The glucose is stored by the liver as insoluble **glycogen** / **glucagon**.

b) One of the ways Ryan controls his diabetes is through exercise. However, while he's out running he steps on some broken glass. A reflex action allows him to react very quickly. Place numbers in the boxes to show the **passage of a reflex**, starting with 'stimulus'.

| ☐ Response | ☐ Sensory neurone | ☐ Receptor |
| ☐ Motor neurone | [1] Stimulus | ☐ Relay neurone |

c) Ryan's foot is hurt badly and an ambulance is called.
Describe how sound from the ambulance siren reaches his ears.

....

....

....

d) **Nerves** carry messages around the body, but they do this in a different way from **hormones**. Put a tick in the table to show whether the characteristic refers to nerve or hormone messages.

Characteristic	Nerve messages	Hormone messages
travel along neurones		
made in glands		
chemical signal		
coordinated by the brain		
travels in the blood		

You've got some nerve stealing my message...

Q2 Jody works in a laboratory that handles **acids**.

a) The **hazard symbol** on the right is on one bottle of acid Jody uses.
What does the symbol mean?

....

b) Name the scale used to measure how acidic a chemical is.

....

c) Write a general word equation to show the reaction between an acid and a metal carbonate.

....

Section 2.3 — My Property

Mixed Questions for Sections 2.1-2.3

Q3 Jane and Roy have three children — Chantelle, Emma and a **new-born** baby daughter called Shakira.

a) Chantelle and Emma are **identical twins**. Tick the correct boxes to show whether the statements below are true or false.

	True	False
i) Jane and Roy are genetically identical.	☐	☐
ii) Genes are the only cause of variation between people.	☐	☐
iii) The twins will have some chromosomes from both of their parents.	☐	☐
iv) The twins will have chromosomes only from their father Roy.	☐	☐

b) Although Chantelle and Emma are identical twins with identical genes, they do not look exactly the same. Explain why this is.

....

....

c) Jane and Roy both have the allele that causes **sickle-cell anaemia**, a disease that affects **red blood cells**. The allele (**a**) that causes the disease is recessive. Complete the Punnett square to show the chance of Jane and Roy's children suffering from the disease.

Take your time when filling in a Punnett square — they're tricky and it's easy to make a mistake.

Jane Aa → A, a

Roy Aa → A, a

	A	a
A	AA	i)
a	ii)	iii)

iv) What **chance** does each child have of having the disorder?

....

d) Shakira has sickle-cell anaemia. Jane and Roy think that **gene therapy** might one day be used to treat her. Are they right? Explain why.

....

....

....

Section 2.3 — My Property

Mixed Questions for Sections 2.1-2.3

Q4 Jack is designing a **new house** for himself.

a) He chooses to use **normal concrete** as one of the building materials.

   i) What four materials make up normal concrete?

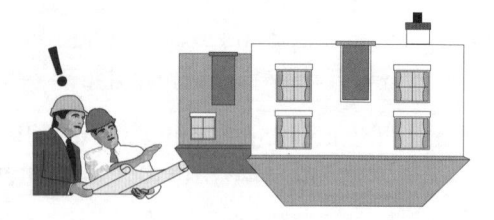

   ....

   ii) Name a **composite** he could use which may be stronger than normal concrete.

   ....

b) Jack chooses to fit **plastic** window frames rather than traditional wooden ones. Give **one** reason why Jack may have chosen to do this.

   ....

c) Jack buys a new kettle for his house. The kettle is metal with a **plastic** handle. Give two properties that the polymer used to make the **handle** will have.

   1. ....

   2. ....

Higher only → d) Jack's new oven burns propane. Complete the symbol equation for the complete combustion of propane.

$$C_3H_8 + 5O_2 \rightarrow 3........... + 4...........$$

Q5 A group of farmers live on a remote Scottish island. The island is very hilly and the weather is often cloudy or rainy. The farmers decide to put up **wind turbines** to generate **electricity**.

a) Suggest why the farmers can **not** rely on the National Grid to provide them with electricity.

   ....

   ....

b) Why might they have chosen to use **wind power** to generate electricity?

   ....

c) i) Suggest one other **renewable energy source** you might advise the farmers to consider.

   ....

   ii) Give one reason the farmers might choose **not** to use this source.

   ....

Section 2.3 — My Property

Mixed Questions for Sections 2.1-2.3

Q6 Emma's job is to install networks into offices using **fibreoptic cables**. These cables carry electromagnetic (EM) waves.

a) Write a **T** or **F** in the box to show if the following statement is **true** or **false**.

EM waves transfer energy and matter from one place to another. ☐

b) A and B are two EM waves used in optical fibres. A has wavelength 850 nanometres and B has a wavelength of 1310 nanometres. (A nanometre is just a very small unit of length.)

i) Which of these two waves has a higher frequency? ....

ii) Which carries more energy? ....

Q7 Matt is trying to choose the best light bulb to use in his bedroom. He studies the information on the box of one light bulb. It gives the potential difference as **20 V** and the current as **0.5 A**.

power = potential difference × current
power = energy transferred ÷ time

a) Calculate the power of the light bulb.

....

....

b) Matt finds a second light bulb that transfers 580 J in one minute. Is this light bulb more powerful than the one in part **a)**?

....

....

c) Matt finally decides on a light bulb that has a power of 9 W. What is this light bulb's power in kW?

....

d) Matt works out that, over the course of a year, he'll be using the light bulb for 1100 hours. How much energy would this light bulb transfer in that time? Give your answer in kWh.

....

....

e) Matt's energy company charges him 11p for each kWh of energy that he uses. How much will it cost for Matt to use the lightbulb for 1100 hours?

....

....

Section 2.3 — My Property

Section 3.1 — Improving Health and Wellbeing

Microorganisms and Disease

Q1 Jackie is an **epidemiologist**, which means she studies outbreaks of disease. Disease can spread by unhygienic conditions or by contact with an infected person.

a) Draw lines to match the descriptions of the diseases with how they are spread.

| Cholera is found in raw sewage | contact with infected people. |
| Flu is found in droplets in the air breathed out by an infected person | unhygienic conditions. |

b) Diseases can enter the body through the respiratory system or by sexual transmission. Give two other ways that diseases can enter the body.

1. ....

2. ....

Q2 **Infectious diseases** are caused by microorganisms like bacteria and viruses.

Tick the boxes to show whether the following diseases are caused by **bacteria** or a **virus**.

	Bacteria	Virus
a) cholera	☐	☐
b) mumps	☐	☐
c) rubella	☐	☐
d) tuberculosis	☐	☐
e) polio	☐	☐

Q3 After eating some **leftovers** that weren't **reheated properly** Ashley has been suffering from **food poisoning**.

a) Food poisoning can be caused by pathogens. What are pathogens?

....

b) Tick the boxes to show whether the following statements are **true** or **false**.

	True	False
i) All bacteria cause disease.	☐	☐
ii) All viruses cause disease.	☐	☐
iii) Pathogens reproduce quickly inside the body.	☐	☐

c) i) Describe how bacteria make you feel ill.

....

ii) Describe how viruses make you feel ill.

....

The Body's Defence Systems

Q1 Sally is a **medical student** studying the ways that the body can **prevent** microorganisms **entering**.

Complete the passage using some of the words given in the box.

> platelets   clot   microorganisms   cells

The skin acts as a barrier to infection. If the skin is broken, e.g. if it is cut, ... can get into the body. ...., which are small fragments of ...., help the blood ...., which seals the wound and prevents infection.

Q2 Sophie is an **immunologist**. She studies how the body destroys different pathogens that enter it.

  a) Circle the correct word(s) in each pair to complete each sentence below.

   i) The **circulatory** / **immune** system attacks microorganisms in the body.

   ii) The **white blood cells** / **platelets** in the body attack microorganisms.

  b) Number the following sentences in the correct order to show how the body can attack an invading pathogen.

   ☐ The antibodies lock on to the antigens and kill the pathogens.

   ☐ Lymphocytes recognise a foreign antigen.

   ☐ Lymphocytes produce antibodies specific to the antigens of the pathogen.

   ☐ If the person is infected with the same pathogen again, the white blood cells will produce antibodies very quickly to prevent the person from getting ill.

  c) i) Name a type of white blood cell, other than a lymphocyte.

   ....

   ii) Describe how the white blood cell you named in part **i)** attacks microbes in the body.

   ....

Top Tips: Make sure you know the difference between antibodies and antigens — it's easy to get them confused. The same goes for the different types of white blood cells — I'll be the first to admit that they've got weird names, but you need to know what each of them does in the body.

Section 3.1 — Improving Health and Wellbeing

Vaccination

Q1 Melissa wants to know **why** vaccines are useful.

Fill in the gaps in the paragraph below using words from the box.

| live | infects | diseases | killed | immune |

You can be vaccinated against some .... so that you become .... to them. If the .... form of the disease .... the body after that, it will be .... immediately.

Q2 Scientists developed a new **vaccine** against **virus Z**. **Twenty people** took part in a **trial** of the vaccine. The results of the trial are shown in the table.

Number of people who became immune to virus Z.	18
Number of people who contracted the illness the next year.	1
Number of people who suffered side effects.	7

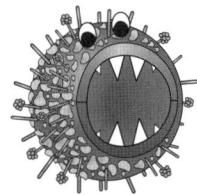

a) Give **two** disadvantages of the new vaccine.

1. ....

2. ....

b) Give one advantage of having a vaccine against virus Z.

....

c) The following statements describe how vaccine Z works but they are in the wrong order. Put numbers in the boxes to show the correct order.

☐ The dead virus Z microorganisms carry antigens so the white blood cells make antibodies against them.

☐ Antibodies are made very quickly and the virus Z microorganisms are killed before they have a chance to make you ill.

☐ If virus Z enters the body again, the white blood cells recognise it straight away.

☐ Dead virus Z is injected into the body.

d) If most people in the UK were vaccinated against virus Z, how would you expect the occurrence of the virus to be affected?

....

....

Section 3.1 — Improving Health and Wellbeing

Use of Drugs to Treat Disease

Q1 Mohan is a **pharmacist**. He dispenses drugs, e.g. antibiotics, to people who are unwell.

a) What are antibiotics?

....

b) Fill in the missing gaps below using words from the box.

antibiotics	aspirin	disease	dangerous

Drugs are .... if misused. Some drugs are used to treat

............................., for example .... (e.g. penicillin)

and anti-inflammatories (e.g. ....).

c) Draw lines to match up the types of drugs with their function.

- painkillers
- antibiotics
- antidepressants

- only relieve the symptoms of disease
- target the cause of disease (the bacteria)

Q2 Ralph thinks his brother takes **sleeping tablets** too often.

a) Circle the correct word(s) to complete the following sentence.

Sleeping tablets **cure** / **relieve the symptoms of** a disease.

b) Give two possible effects of someone over-using drugs such as sleeping tablets.

1. ....

2. ....

c) Ralph once took sleeping tablets but he had a bad reaction to them.

Tick the boxes to show whether the following statements are **true** or **false**.   True   False

i) People's genes have an effect on how they react to drugs.   ☐   ☐

ii) Personalised drugs should reduce bad reactions to drugs.   ☐   ☐

iii) Personalising drugs is a quick and cheap process.   ☐   ☐

Section 3.1 — Improving Health and Wellbeing

Antibiotic Resistance and Drug Testing

Q1 A pharmaceutical company has developed a **new medicine** which has to undergo clinical trials before being made available to the public.

   a) Explain what a clinical trial is.

   ....

   b) Before a medicine undergoes a clinical trial, it has to be tested in other ways. Circle the correct options below to show what the medicine would be tested on **before** a clinical trial.

   hair samples   cells   tissues

   plant tissues   animals   human patients

   c) Tick the boxes to show whether the following statements are **true** or **false**.   True   False

   i) Drugs that are approved for sale are monitored for safety for one further year.   ☐ ☐

   ii) Drugs that are approved for sale are monitored for safety for five further years.   ☐ ☐

   iii) Drugs that are approved for sale are monitored for safety throughout their use.   ☐ ☐

Higher only

Q2 a) Write numbers in the boxes below to show the **order** the statements should be in to explain how bacteria become resistant to antibiotics. The first one has been done for you.

   | 1 | Bacteria mutate and sometimes the mutations cause them to be resistant to an antibiotic.
   | ☐ | The population of the resistant strain of bacteria will increase.
   | ☐ | When you treat the infection, only the non-resistant strains of bacteria will be killed.
   | ☐ | The individual resistant bacteria will survive and reproduce.
   | ☐ | So if you have an infection, some of the bacteria might be resistant to antibiotics.

   b) Name **one** type of bacterium that has developed resistance to antibiotics.

   ....

   c) Sandy has a mild throat infection.

   i) Do you think that Sandy's doctor would prescribe antibiotics to treat the infection?

   ....

   ii) Explain your answer.

   ....

   ....

Top Tips: It takes years for a drug to reach the general public. It has to go through loads of different stages to make sure it is effective and has no serious side effects.

Section 3.1 — Improving Health and Wellbeing

Recreational Drugs

Q1 Legal and illegal drugs can be used **recreationally**. There are many harmful effects of these drugs.

a) Name **two** legal recreational drugs.

1. ....

2. ....

b) Draw lines to link the drugs below to their correct descriptions.

Antidepressants	Medical drugs used to make you sleep
Amphetamine	Stimulants designed to reduce depression
Nicotine	Stimulant drug — its common name is speed
Barbiturates	Addictive drug found in cigarettes

c) Fill in the blanks in the paragraph using words from the box below.

need   withdrawal   chemical   addictive   physical

Drugs change some of the .... processes in the body. Most drugs that are used recreationally can be ...., meaning that the person can have a .... need for the drug. If they don't have the drug they might get .... symptoms.

d) The misuse of recreational drugs can have harmful physical and psychological effects. Circle the recreational drugs below that are **illegal**.

cannabis   tobacco   alcohol   barbiturates   cocaine   heroin   amphetamines

e) Give two impacts that illegal recreational drugs can have on the body.

....

....

Section 3.1 — Improving Health and Wellbeing

Recreational Drugs

Q2 A **drug counsellor** is discussing the **effects of alcohol** with an addict.

a) Drinking alcohol in excess can cause damage to the body.
Fill in the blanks in the paragraph using words from the box below.

| liver | nervous | brain | unconsciousness |

Drinking alcohol reduces the activity of the .... system.

Alcohol in excess can cause .... It can also damage

brain cells, causing a noticeable drop in .... function.

Too much alcohol can also cause severe damage to the ....

b) Suggest **two** reasons why it is dangerous to drink and drive.

....

....

Q3 Anthony and his doctor are talking about why he should stop **smoking**.

a) Circle the correct word(s) in each pair to complete the paragraph describing the effects of smoking on the **circulatory system**.

Cigarettes contain carbon monoxide, which **reduces** / **increases** the
amount of **oxygen** / **nitrogen** that the blood can carry. Smoking
also causes disease of the **stomach** / **heart** and blood vessels.
This can lead to **heart attacks** / **liver disease** and **cancer** / **strokes**.

b) Give one disease of the **respiratory system** that is caused by tobacco smoke.

....

c) Anthony is addicted to the nicotine in cigarettes. What effect would he feel if he stops smoking?

....

Top Tips: Both legal and illegal drugs can have a major impact on your body. Drugs can also be addictive and cause antisocial behaviour, especially when used in excess. Alcohol's one of the most common legal drugs around but it still causes some really serious problems — so if you're going to use it, do it in moderation. And as for the illegal drugs, it's really not worth getting involved.

Section 3.1 — Improving Health and Wellbeing

Medical Uses of Radiation

Q1 a) Complete the following table on **types of radiation**.

Type of radiation	Nature of radiation	Absorbed by... Paper	Absorbed by... Thin sheet of aluminium	Absorbed by... Thick concrete
Alpha	....	✓	✓	....
....	particles	✗	....	....
Gamma	....	....	....	....

b) Gamma rays are used to diagnose and treat some illnesses. Complete the following paragraph on **gamma rays** using the words provided.

> gamma   kill   cells   tumour   cancer   radioactive

A .... tracer can be injected into a person. The tracer will build up in a certain part of the body, e.g. in a .... , and give out gamma rays. The gamma rays can be detected using a .... camera — the image created can be used to diagnose diseases in the body. High doses of gamma rays will .... living .... Because of this, gamma rays are used to treat ....

Q2 Ranjit is a **radiographer** who takes **X-rays** of people to see if they have any broken bones.

a) Give two characteristics of X-ray waves.

1. ....

2. ....

b) On the right is an X-ray photograph of a hand.

   i) Label with an X on the diagram where fewer X-rays have passed through the person's body on to the photographic plate.

   ii) Why can you see **bone** but not **flesh** in the X-ray?

   ....

   ....

   iii) What other material would show up on an X-ray?

   ....

Section 3.1 — Improving Health and Wellbeing

Radiation Safety Precautions and Ethics

Q1 Michael is a **radiographer** at a large hospital. He spends a lot of his time at work taking **X-rays** of patients.

a) Michael has to wear a **film badge** at work. Use the words given to label the diagram of a film badge below.

photographic film   plastic casing   metal filter

i) ....

ii) ....   iii) ....

b) Describe what a film badge monitors.

....

c) Explain why Michael has to wear a film badge.

....

....

Q2 Julia has **breast cancer** and is being treated with **radiotherapy** by her doctors.

Describe **one** ethical issue that Julie and her doctors would have considered before starting her radiotherapy treatment.

....

....

Top Tips: Radiation is everywhere, but some types of radiation are more dangerous than others. Strangely enough, the radiation that's used in hospitals is the most deadly. It's important that people working with radiation monitor how much they're exposed to so they can protect themselves.

Section 3.1 — Improving Health and Wellbeing

Section 3.2 — Developing and Improving Products

Electroplating

Q1 Household objects are often electroplated. Explain what is meant by the term '**electroplating**'.

....

....

Q2 **Draw lines** between the boxes below to link the words with their descriptions. The words may be linked to **more than one** description.

- cathode
- anode
- ion
- electrolyte

- the negative electrode — it's the object that is being electroplated
- an atom that has lost or gained electrons
- a charged particle that moves through the electrolyte during electroplating
- metal atoms are deposited on it
- a solution of the metal ions used for plating
- the positive electrode — it's usually a bar of the metal used for plating

Q3 Arjun is electroplating his paperclip collection with silver. He wants to find out what's actually happening at the **electrodes**.

a) **Underline** the correct word from each pair to complete the following sentences.

i) Metal atoms at the anode **gain / lose** electrons, and become **positively charged / neutral** metal **ions / atoms**.

ii) Metal ions at the cathode **gain / lose** electrons, and become **positively charged / neutral** metal **ions / atoms**.

b) Complete the following equations, showing exactly what's going on at each electrode.

i) At the **anode**: Ag → .... + ...

ii) At the **cathode**: .... + e⁻ → ....

Uses and Risks of Electroplating

Q1 Electroplating is used for several **different purposes**.

Complete the passage about **decorative** electroplating below using the words provided.

nickel   gold   jewellery   allergies   shiny

Decorative items like .... are often electroplated with

silver or .... to make them look ....

Jewellery is sometimes made out of .... (a cheap metal) and

is electroplated to make it look nicer and to prevent ....

Q2 Some metal items in Tim's home have been electroplated to **prevent corrosion**.

a) Circle the correct word(s) to show one type of **household item** that is often electroplated to **prevent corrosion**.

jewellery   cutlery   electrical wires   glass

b) Give an example of a **metal** that could be used to electroplate the item you circled in part **a)**.

....

c) Explain **why** the metal you gave as your answer to part **b)** is a suitable choice.

....

....

Q3 Lilia works in an electroplating factory. Give two **potential dangers** she is faced with at work.

1. ....

....

2. ....

....

Top Tips: This stuff on electroplating is really important. Whether or not you've got your heart set on a career in the electroplating industry, you'll need to know it all for your exam. And don't forget, making things shiny and pretty by electroplating them can be quite dangerous.

Section 3.2 — Developing and Improving Products

New Products

Q1 Molly's new car has been coated with a self-healing **smart paint**.

a) Tick the box next to the statement below that best describes the paint on Molly's car.

| The paint changes colour, depending on the temperature. | ☐ |

| The paint returns to a 'remembered shape' when it's heated up. | ☐ |

| The paint can repair scratches in its surface when it's exposed to sunlight. | ☐ |

b) Explain how this smart paint could save Molly money.

....

....

c) Give **one** disadvantage of smart paints like the one on Molly's new car.

....

d) Give **one** other application of self-healing smart paint.

....

Make sure you learn the uses of all the different types of smart materials.

Q2 Under normal conditions **all** metals have **electrical resistance**.

a) Circle the correct word(s) to complete the sentence below.

A superconductor is a material that has almost zero / high **electrical resistance.**

b) Give one **advantage** of superconductors.

....

c) Give two possible **uses** of superconductors.

1. ....

2. ....

d) Explain a **drawback** of using today's superconductors.

....

....

Section 3.2 — Developing and Improving Products

New Products

Q3 Some metals can return to a 'remembered shape' when they are heated to a certain temperature.

a) Explain why these metals are 'smart materials'.

....

....

b) Give two things these metals could be used to make.

1. ....

2. ....

Q4 The packaging around some **fresh meat** has a coloured dot on it that gradually gets **darker**. The **speed** at which this happens depends on the **temperature**, as shown in this graph.

a) When the dot is more than **80% dark**, the food is no longer safe to eat. The graph shows that when kept at **5 °C**, the food is safe to eat for up to **80 hours**. For how long is it safe to eat when kept at:

i) 15 °C? ....

ii) 25 °C? ....

b) Circle the correct word to show the name given to materials that change colour in different conditions.

   chromic materials   memory materials

c) Give the name of this type of packaging.

   photochromic material   intelligent packaging   recyclable packaging

d) Explain why this type of packaging is useful.

....

....

e) The meat is shrink wrapped using a different type of smart material. Explain how the meat could be shrink wrapped using a smart material.

....

....

....

Section 3.2 — Developing and Improving Products

Selective Breeding

Q1 Jeremy is a **beef farmer**. To increase his profits, he **selectively breeds** cows that have the highest meat yields.

a) Number the sentences below to show the stages of selective breeding in the correct order.

- [ ] Breed them with each other (cross-breeding).
- [ ] Select the best offspring.
- [ ] Continue the process over many generations.
- [ ] Combine with the best you already have and breed again.
- [1] Select individuals with the best characteristics.

b) Complete the following sentences by circling the correct word(s) in each pair.

i) Selective breeding **increases** / **decreases** the number of variations of a gene in a population.

ii) Animals in a herd that have been bred selectively will be **closely** / **distantly** related.

iii) If a new disease appears **few** / **all** of the animals are likely to be affected.

iv) There's **more** / **less** chance of organisms developing genetic diseases.

Q2 Sarah has just inherited a **dairy farm**. A local farmer has offered her a choice of bulls to **breed** with her cows.

a) Circle **two** characteristics that Sarah should look for in the bulls.

Good disease resistance   High milk yield in the bull's mother   Bad-tempered   Low fertility

b) The graph shows the milk yield for Sarah's cows over the last three generations.

The average milk yield per cow is the highest point on each line.

i) What was the average milk yield per cow for generation 1?

....

ii) What was the **increase** in the average milk yield per cow from generation 1 to generation 3?

....

iii) Do you think that **selective breeding** has been used with these cows? Explain your answer.

....
....
....

Section 3.2 — Developing and Improving Products

Tissue Culture and Cloning

Q1 Clive **clones** some plants to produce new offspring.

a) **Circle** the correct words to complete the passage below.

> Clones are genetically **different** / **identical** organisms or **cells** / **plants**. Scientists can clone plants **and** / **but not** animals. The technique used in laboratories is called **nutrient medium** / **tissue culture**.

b) Tick the boxes to say whether the following are **true** or **false**.

	True	False
i) The offspring are genetically identical to each other.	☐	☐
ii) The offspring are genetically identical to their parent.	☐	☐
iii) The offspring are genetically different from their parent and each other.	☐	☐

Q2 Kim works for a large **research** firm. One of the tasks she carries out on a daily basis is **cloning** of maize plants. The diagram below shows the process of producing **cloned maize plants**.

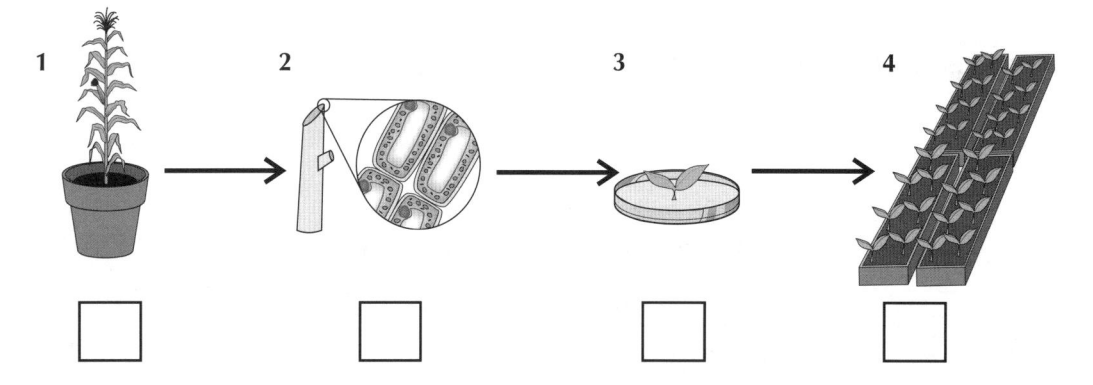

1   2   3   4

a) Match the following statements to the stages in the diagram by writing the letter in the correct box.

- **A** Cells removed from the plant.
- **B** Clones grown in potting compost.
- **C** Parent plant with desired characteristics.
- **D** Cells placed on a jelly containing nutrients.

b) The company Kim works for also carries out tissue culture using **animal tissue**.

The following statement is incorrect: "It's possible to culture single cells or populations of cells but not whole organs". Write out a **corrected** version of the statement.

....

....

Section 3.2 — Developing and Improving Products

Genetic Engineering

Q1 **Scientists** can use **genetic engineering** to modify organisms. Complete the passage below using words in the box to describe genetic engineering.

| characteristics | animals | foreign | plants | early | desired |

Bacteria, ... and .... can all be genetically engineered. The genes that are transferred are sometimes called .... genes. The transfer must be done in the very .... stages of development so that it develops with the .... characteristics. The .... that the genetically modified (GM) organism has depends on the type of gene inserted.

Q2 Heather is a member of a group that campaigns **against** genetically engineered foods.

a) Suggest **two** reasons why Heather might think that genetic engineering is **ethically** wrong.

1. ....
....
2. ....
....

b) Tick **two** advantages of genetic engineering.
- ☐ The gene used could escape.
- ☐ Crops could be produced with added vitamins.
- ☐ Crops could be produced to be more susceptible to disease.
- ☐ Animals could be produced that would grow more quickly.

Q3 Explain how genetic engineering can be used to make human insulin.

....
....
....

Top Tips: Genetic engineering is tricky stuff. It's got the potential to be really useful in all sorts of ways, but there are lots of ethical problems linked to genetically engineered organisms and genetically modified food. Make sure you know about them.

Section 3.2 — Developing and Improving Products

Greenhouse Gases

Q1 Scientists are concerned that **human activity** is **increasing** the levels of **greenhouse gases** in the atmosphere. Circle the correct words in each pair to show how this is happening.

a) Household rubbish breaking down in landfill sites increases the level of **methane / water** in the atmosphere.

b) Burning **fossil fuels / hydrogen** increases the level of **carbon dioxide / oxygen** in the atmosphere.

c) Power stations are increasing the level of carbon dioxide and **methane / nitrous oxide** in the atmosphere.

d) The increased use of **nitrogen-based fertilisers / chemical pesticides** is increasing the level of nitrous oxide in the atmosphere.

e) Growing rice in watery fields increases the level of **methane / nitrous oxide** in the atmosphere.

Q2 Finn is an **environmental scientist**. He's studying how the amount of **nitrous oxide** (a greenhouse gas) produced by **motor vehicles** changes over time. The graph below shows some of his results.

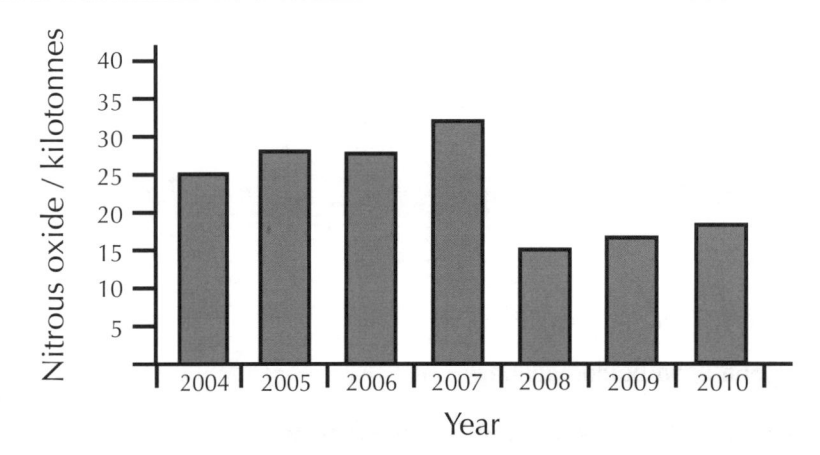

a) Circle the correct word from each pair to complete the passage below and describe the trend shown in the graph.

The amount of nitrous oxide in the air **increased / dropped** from 2004

to 2007, then **increased / dropped**, then began to **increase / drop** again.

b) A new **bypass** was recently built that bypassed the area studied. Use the graph to suggest which year it was finished.

....

c) Nitrous oxide is also produced by **bacteria** in soils. Give the name of this process.

....

d) Name **one other** greenhouse gas produced by motor vehicles that Finn could study.

....

Section 3.3 — Environmental Concerns

Global Warming and The Kyoto Agreement

Q1 Professor Gilbert is giving a lecture to some students about **global warming**. He's explaining to the students why the **increase** in **greenhouse gases** is causing global warming.

a) Explain the term 'global warming'.

....

b) Complete the paragraph below using the words in the box to fill in the gaps.

atmosphere greenhouse heat Sun more

Greenhouse gases in the Earth's .... help to keep the planet warm by absorbing energy from the ....
This energy is in the form of long-wave radiation. Increasing levels of
.... gases mean that .... energy is absorbed and more .... is trapped.
This is causing global warming.

Q2 The Minister for the Environment is explaining the importance of the **Kyoto Agreement** to a group of school children.

a) Tick the box to show which of the following statements about the Kyoto Agreement is **correct**.

A The Kyoto Agreement is an agreement on what to do about water pollution. ☐

B The Kyoto Agreement is an agreement on what to do about climate change. ☐

C The Kyoto Agreement won't affect levels of greenhouse gases. ☐

D The Kyoto Agreement is an agreement between the countries of Europe only. ☐

b) Describe the main aim of the Kyoto Agreement.

....

....

c) i) Name **one** country that refused to sign the Kyoto Agreement.

....

ii) Suggest why this refusal might make the Kyoto Agreement **less effective**.

....

....

Section 3.3 — Environmental Concerns

Pollution

Q1 Paul is a **farmer**. Some of the **artificial chemicals** he uses on his farm can cause pollution in **lakes** and **rivers**.

Name the three types of chemical that can cause this pollution.

1. ....

2. ....

3. ....

Q2 Nigel works for the **Environment Agency**. He's investigating reports that a **stream** (which runs alongside a farmer's land) has become covered in a thick layer of **algae**.

a) Suggest a **chemical** used in farming that could be the cause of this algal growth.

....

b) The chemical enters the water by a process known as **leaching**.
Explain what is meant by the word leaching.

....

....

c) i) Put the following sentences in order to describe the problems that this algal growth will cause. The first one has been done for you.

☐ Fish die.

[1] Layer of algae blocks out sunlight.

☐ Decomposers feed on dead plants.

☐ Plants die.

☐ All the oxygen in the water is used up.

ii) Give the **name** of this process.

....

Top Tips: You really do need to know about the problems that algal growth causes and the order these problems happen in — it's just the sort of thing examiners love to test you on. So learn it.

Section 3.3 — Environmental Concerns

Pollution and Indicator Species

Q1 Juanita is studying **sludgeworms** in her local river to see how much **sewage** is in the water.

a) Give the **name** given to organisms that are used in this way.

....

Juanita recorded the number of **sludgeworms** in water samples taken at three different distances away from a **sewage outlet**. Her results are shown below.

Distance (km)	No. of sludgeworms
1	20
2	14
3	7

b) Explain what you can tell about the sludgeworm from these results.

....

c) Name **two** other organisms that Juanita could have studied to look at **water pollution**.

....

Q2 Amanda has collected samples of **dead organisms** from a pond.
She analyses them for the presence of **pesticides**.
The diagram below shows the **concentrations** of pesticide Amanda found in each organism.

ppm means parts per million

Concentration of pesticide in microscopic algae: 0.05 ppm → Concentration of pesticide in microscopic animals: 4 ppm → Concentration of pesticide in small fish: 500 ppm → Concentration of pesticide in eels: 2500 ppm

a) Suggest **where** the pesticide in the pond might have come from.

....

b) Calculate how many times more **concentrated** the pesticide was in eels compared to in the microscopic algae.

....

c) Only a low concentration of pesticide was present in the water.
Explain why the concentration of pesticide in eels is so **high**.

....

....

Section 3.3 — Environmental Concerns

Waste Disposal and Plastics

Q1 Alan **doesn't recycle** his plastic bottles — he puts them in the rubbish bin. Some of these bottles will end up in a **landfill site**. Others will be **incinerated**.

a) Name **one** problem with landfill sites.

....

b) i) Describe what happens to waste when it is incinerated.

....

ii) Give **one** problem with incinerating plastics.

....

Q2 Ash is the manager of a rubbish tip. He's thinking of offering **plastic recycling** facilities, but before he invests he wants to weigh up the **pros** and **cons**.

Give **one** advantage and **one** disadvantage of recycling plastics.

Advantage: ....

Disadvantage: ....

Q3 (Higher only) Helen is designing **plastic carrier bags** for a large supermarket chain. The supermarket wants the bags to be more environmentally friendly. She's chosen to make them out of a **biodegradable plastic**.

a) Explain why **biodegradable plastics** are better for the environment than **non-biodegradable** ones.

....

....

....

....

b) Helen is trying to decide between a **photo-degradable** plastic and a **water-soluble** plastic.

i) Explain what **water-soluble** means.

....

ii) Explain how **photo-degradable plastic** breaks down.

....

iii) Name **one water-soluble plastic** that Helen could use.

....

Section 3.3 — Environmental Concerns

Heat Loss in the Home

Q1 a) Indicate whether each of the following statements is true or false.

       True False

   i) Heat energy can be transferred by radiation, conduction and convection. ☐ ☐

   ii) Conduction involves the transfer of energy between moving particles. ☐ ☐

   iii) Radiation is where objects take in energy from their surroundings. ☐ ☐

   iv) Convection always involves a moving liquid or gas. ☐ ☐

   v) Metal objects (e.g. saucepans) do not conduct heat. ☐ ☐

b) For each of the following, state which **type** of heat transfer is happening.

   i) Warm air at the bottom of a room rising to the top.

   ....

   ii) The handle of a metal spoon heating up after it's been put in a cup of tea.

   ....

   iii) The Sun warming the Earth.

   ....

Q2 Gary is choosing between three brands of loft insulation material. The **U-values** of the three brands are shown in the table below.

	U-value
Brand A	0.15
Brand B	0.20
Brand C	0.19

a) Explain what U-values show.

....

b) If all three brands are the same price, suggest which brand should Gary buy. Explain your answer.

....

....

....

Top Tips: U-values — loads of fun. You need to know what they're used to show and the difference between high and low U-values. Don't forget about the three types of heat transfer either...

Section 3.3 — Environmental Concerns

Reducing Heat Loss in the Home

Q1 Heat is lost from a house through its **roof**, **walls**, **doors** and **windows**. In the spaces on the diagram below, write down one measure that could be taken to reduce heat losses through each part of the house.

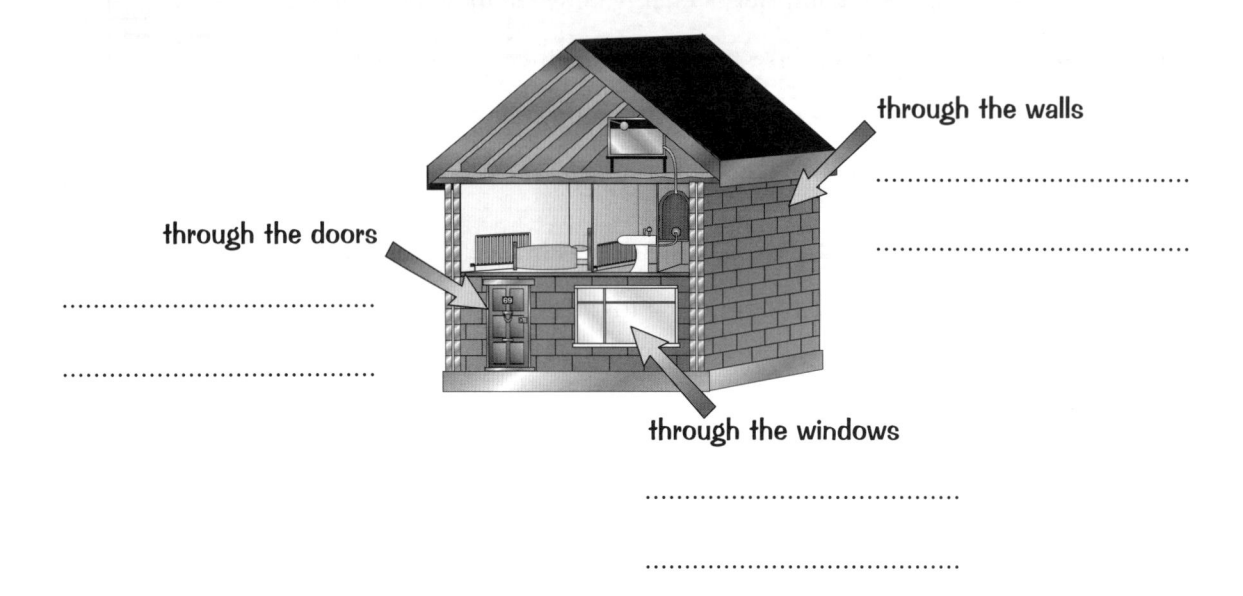

through the walls
....
....

through the doors
....
....

through the windows
....
....

Q2 Mr Tarantino wants to buy **double glazing** for his house. The salesman tries to sell him insulated window shutters instead. He says it is cheaper and more **cost-effective**.

	Double glazing	Insulated window shutters
Initial Cost	£3000	£1700
Annual Saving	£60	£20
Payback time	50 years	

a) Calculate the **payback time** for insulated shutters and write it in the table.

$$\text{payback time} = \frac{\text{initial cost}}{\text{annual saving}}$$

b) Suggest whether the salesman's advice is correct. Give reasons for your answer.

....
....

c) Are **efficiency** and **cost-effectiveness** are the same thing? Explain your answer.

....
....
....

Section 3.3 — Environmental Concerns

Pollutants in the Home

Q1 Hannah is researching the effects of **pollutants** in the **home**. She's worried about the effects they might have on both her and her daughter's health.

a) Which of the following are pollutants in the home? Circle the correct answers.

    dust   pollen   lemon juice   children   toilet bleach

b) Name three **health problems** that pollutants in the home can cause.

1. ....

2. ....

3. ....

c) Hannah notices the symbol on the right on the label of the product she uses to clean her bathroom.

   i) Write down what this symbol means.

      ....

      ....

The hazard symbols on cleaning products are the same as the ones you'd find on chemicals in the lab.

   ii) Describe **two** things that Hannah could do to **reduce** the **risk** of using this product.

      ....

      ....

d) Suggest **one** thing Hannah could do to **reduce pollution** in her home.

....

Q2 The concentration of **radon** gas found in people's homes varies across the UK.

a) Explain why the concentration varies across the country.

....

b) Explain why high concentrations of radon are dangerous.

....

c) Suggest how people in high radon areas can reduce the radon concentration in their homes.

....

Section 3.3 — Environmental Concerns

Domestic Boilers

Q1 Dan is having a **new boiler** fitted in his house. His old boiler was broken and **incomplete combustion** was happening inside it.

a) Which of the following does a domestic boiler need to work efficiently? Circle the correct answer.

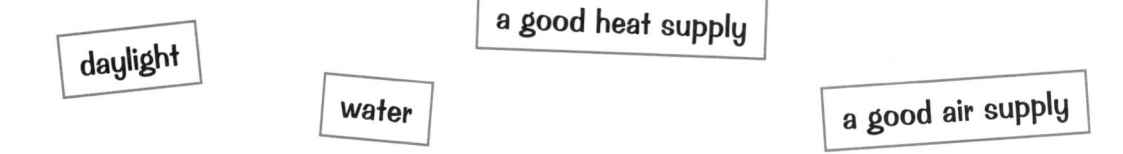

daylight   water   a good heat supply   a good air supply

b) Complete the equation below to show the reaction that was taking place inside Dan's **old** boiler.

fuel + ... → soot + ... + carbon dioxide + water

Q2 Sarah called out an engineer because her boiler wasn't working as efficiently as it was meant to. The engineer said it was because of **incomplete combustion**.

a) Write down what combustion is.
....

b) Explain when incomplete combustion takes place.
....

c) Name a **toxic product** that can be released by incomplete combustion in a boiler.
....

d) i) Describe how incomplete combustion affects the **energy output** of a domestic boiler.
....

ii) Explain why this is.
....
....

Incomplete combustion

Top Tips: The humble domestic boiler. Where would we be without it, eh? Apart from huddled together under a heap of duvets struggling to stay warm. You really do need to know all this stuff. It'll help you in the exam — and in life. Worth getting your head around, I'd say.

Section 3.3 — Environmental Concerns

Mixed Questions for Sections 3.1-3.3

Q1 Larry has made a **New Year's resolution** to become more **healthy**. He asks his doctor for advice. His doctor suggests he should give up **smoking** and reduce the amount of **alcohol** he drinks.

a) Suggest **one** reason why Larry might find it difficult to give up smoking.

....

b) **Carbon monoxide** is found in tobacco smoke. What effect does this chemical have on the body?

....

c) Circle the correct word(s) in each pair to complete each sentence below about alcohol.

i) Alcohol **speeds up** / **slows down** your reaction time.

ii) Drinking lots of alcohol damages your **brain and liver** / **eye and nose** cells.

iii) Alcohol is a recreational drug that's **legal** / **illegal**.

d) Larry occasionally takes **cocaine**, an illegal recreational drug.

i) Should Larry stop taking cocaine to improve his health? Give **one** reason for your answer.

....

....

ii) Name one other illegal recreational drug.

....

Q2 James is feeling **ill** and thinks that he must have an **infection**. He goes to see a doctor.

a) The doctor tells James that he has **influenza**, which is a viral infection. Name **two** other illnesses caused by viruses.

1. ....   2. ....

b) Give two ways that white blood cells respond to viruses and other pathogens entering the body.

1. ....

2. ....

c) How could James have reduced his chances of being infected with influenza?

....

d) Tick the boxes to show whether the following statements about viruses are **true** or **false**.

                                                                                      True False

i) Viruses are killed by antibiotics.

ii) Viruses usually damage body cells when they replicate.

Section 3.3 — Environmental Concerns

Mixed Questions for Sections 3.1-3.3

Q3 The lenses in Marta's glasses are made from a **photochromic smart material**.

a) Tick the correct box to show which statement describes a **photochromic** material.

A photochromic material changes colour in response to changes in light intensity. ☐

A photochromic material changes colour in response to changes in temperature. ☐

b) Name **three** other products that use photochromic materials.

1. ....

2. ....

3. ....

c) Name **two other** types of smart material.

1. ....

2. ....

Q4 Garfield wants to breed one type of plant for its **fruit**, and another as a **house plant**.

a) Suggest a characteristic that he should select for in each kind of plant.

i) Fruit plant: ....

ii) House plant: ....

b) One of Garfield's plants has the characteristics he wants. He decides to clone it.

i) Circle the correct word to show a laboratory technique that he could use.

genetic engineering   tissue culture   selective breeding

ii) Describe how this method can produce clones of a parent plant.

....

....

....

c) Explain why Garfield chose to reproduce his plant by cloning.

....

....

Section 3.3 — Environmental Concerns

Mixed Questions for Sections 3.1-3.3

Q5 Albert farms sheep. He wants to **increase** the amount of **wool** his sheep grow. He's looking into whether to do this by **cloning**, **selective breeding** or **genetic engineering**.

a) **Tick** the boxes to say whether the following are **true** or **false**.

                                                                                                True   False

   i) Selective breeding produces offspring who are genetically identical to their parents.

   ii) Only plants can be cloned.

   iii) Selective breeding does not affect the gene pool.

   iv) Cloning is where a gene is transferred from one organism into another.

   v) Genetic engineering has to be done in the very early stages of an organism's development so that it develops with the desired characteristics.

b) Albert decides to increase his sheep's wool production by selective breeding. Give one **disadvantage** of selective breeding.

....

....

Q6 Below are some statements that different people have made about **genetically modified (GM) plants**. In each case, say whether they are making an argument **for** or **against** GM technology.

a) **Genes inserted into crop plants, for example for pest-resistance, may spread to nearby wild plants.**

....

b) **Some people could develop allergic reactions to foods that have been genetically modified.**

....

c) **We can produce rice plants containing toxins that are harmful to locusts but not to people.**

....

d) **By using herbicide-resistant crops on my land, I can kill all the weeds in my field with a single dose of all-purpose herbicide.**

....

e) **Investing in improving traditional agricultural methods will improve yields more than investment in GM technology.**

....

Top Tips: So, if you wanted to take over the world using goldfish, you would probably want to breed together the more aggressive goldfish with long memories, rather than the dappy ones that just idly swim around in a circle all day long. (You can tell which ones are aggressive — they bite.)

Section 3.3 — Environmental Concerns

Mixed Questions for Sections 3.1-3.3

Q7 Paul is looking to buy some cavity wall insulation to reduce heat loss from his house.

a) What is insulation?

....

....

b) i) Should Paul look for cavity wall insulation with a high or a low U-value?

....

ii) Explain your answer.

....

Q8 Erik investigates ways of saving energy in his grandma's house. He calculates the annual savings that could be made on his grandma's fuel bills, and the cost of doing the work.

Work needed	Annual Saving (£)	Cost of work (£)	Money saved over five years (£)
Hot water tank jacket	20	20	(5 × annual saving) - cost of work = (5 × 20) - 20 = 80
Draught-proofing	70	80	
Cavity wall insulation	85	650	
Thermostatic controls	30	140	

a) i) Complete the table to show the amount of money saved by each item over five years.

ii) Write down the option from the table that would save Erik's grandma the most money over 5 years.

....

b) Erik also decides to get his grandma's boiler serviced to make sure it's working efficiently. Explain what would happen in a boiler that wasn't working efficiently.

....

....

....

Section 3.3 — Environmental Concerns